The Kids 'N' Clay Ceramics Book

The Kids 'N' Clay

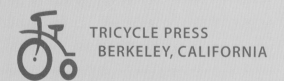

TRICYCLE PRESS
BERKELEY, CALIFORNIA

Ceramics Book

**HANDBUILDING AND WHEEL-THROWING PROJECTS
FROM THE KIDS 'N' CLAY POTTERY STUDIO**

Created by Kevin Nierman
Written by Elaine Arima
Illustrated by Curtis H. Arima

First printing, 2000.
Printed in China
3 4 5 6 7 — 09 08 07 06 05

TRICYCLE PRESS
P.O. Box 7123
Berkeley, California 94707
www.tenspeed.com

Library of Congress Cataloging-in-Publication Data

The Kids 'N' Clay ceramics book : handbuilding and
wheelthrowing projects from the Kids 'N' Clay Pottery
Studio / created by Kevin Nierman ; written by Elaine
Arima ; illustrated by Curtis H. Arima
       p. cm.
    Summary: Teaches basic ceramic techniques and
provides step-by-step instructions for a variety of
projects including handbuilt items, sculptures, and
creations using a potter's wheel.
    ISBN-13: 978-1-883672-89-8 (alk. paper)
    ISBN-10: 1-883672-89-9 (alk. paper)
    1. Pottery craft—Juvenile literature. [1. Pottery
craft. 2. Handicraft.] I. Nierman, Kevin. II. Arima,
Elaine. III. Arima, Curtis H., ill.
TT921 .N54 2000
738—dc21   99-045683

ACKNOWLEDGMENTS

Over the years, several key people have greatly influenced the teachings at Kids 'N' Clay™ and the making of this book. Thank you Faye and Don Nierman for modeling the importance of art and creativity. Thank you Karl Goldstein, for being the mentor who made the teachings at Kids 'N' Clay possible. Thank you Carol Robinson, for being a truly inspiring ceramics teacher. And to all the children and parents who have attended classes, supported, and promoted Kids 'N' Clay over the years, thank you all for making this book a reality.

This book was a creative and collaborative effort that involved the expertise, knowledge, and support of many people behind the scenes. Thank you Dave Larson, our digital photo wizard, for your tireless support and for always being there. Thanks also to Peter Patron for your constant love and encouragement.

Two generous people, Nancy and Steve Selvin, have been never-ending in their support and advice, and have greatly influenced the success of the Kids 'N' Clay Studio.

Gratitude to Sue Bender for seeing the vision, and sharing it with the world, and to the Mason-Gordon family for their continual loving support.

Thank you Curtis H. Arima, our illustrator, for the hundreds of detailed drawings that are shown throughout the book.

Special appreciation to Alissa Kaplan, our primary advisor and reviewer, who proofed and refined the projects in the manuscript.

Other advisors and reviewers who gave us great insights include John Toki and staff, Lauren Webb, Erica Garcia, Diane Spangler, and Si and Ron Arima. Thank you all for your time and valuable suggestions.

Most importantly, we'd like to thank all the Kids 'N' Clay students and others who contributed projects or quotes in this book, and to the staff at Kids 'N' Clay for their hard work and dedication.

We would also like to thank Nicole Geiger, Nancy Austin, Cybele Knowles, and the other team members at Ten Speed Press for the guidance and support they have provided in the development and production of our first book. To the many other friends and family members who have inspired and influenced us along the way, thank you for helping us move forward with our dreams!

CONTENTS

●●●●●●●●●●●●●●●●●

2. Handbuilding Projects 11

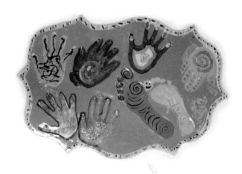

FOREWORD

. . . .

My job is to help kids express themselves, so they can find their own creative paths. There is something very magical about children when they are thinking and working creatively. As a children's ceramics teacher and the owner of Kids 'N' Clay Pottery Studio, I witness this creative transformation every day. Clay is a wonderful, tactile medium that many kids have never experienced before. Its three-dimensional nature forces them to think about structure, shapes, and forms. They can experiment with a variety of building techniques, while learning to think through their ideas and to adapt to change along the way. Once children learn to express and execute their personal visions in clay, they can become empowered in ways that go far beyond the walls of their ceramic studio or a classroom.

I believe that children should not be limited in finding their potential. Ultimately, it doesn't matter whether your child creates cups and plates to use at the dinner table or an exotic sculpture to display in the living room. What does matter is that your child enjoys the creative process and takes pride in sharing personal creations. When children are in a safe environment where they are encouraged to express themselves freely, without limitations, that's when they discover their unique creativity. When they are open to new ideas and experiences, they can create anything in their lives!

—Kevin Nierman

A NOTE TO PARENTS & TEACHERS

The Kids 'N' Clay Ceramics Book is a hands-on lesson in creativity that is based on my 14-plus years of experience as a children's ceramic teacher and a professional artist. This book is my personal way of expressing my passion for ceramics and inspiring more children to explore their creative abilities through clay. By sharing my teaching style and the experiences of my young students, I hope to bring the creative spirit of Kids 'N' Clay Pottery Studio into your child's life. However, this will only be possible with your participation and guidance.

The Importance of Your Role

Your most valuable role as an adult is to be your child's coach and cheerleader. Your positive guidance will be an essential ingredient in your child's creative development, especially when they are experiencing something new. Please assure them that *there is no such thing as a wrong project.* There are only some basic safety rules and building techniques to learn. It's amazing how quickly the feeling of success can transform a child's apprehension into excitement and enthusiastic self-confidence.

But most important, always remember that, as a parent or a teacher, you are only there to facilitate the process. The child is the artist and the creator. It's important for them to make their own decisions and mistakes, as part of the creative process. Try to hold back your urge to fix the problem, unless you are asked to help. Children often see the world through different eyes. What looks like something to them, may not look like anything to you, but what your child sees and learns is all that really matters!

How to Use This Book

This book is designed to simulate the activities and the experiences that are taught at the Kids 'N' Clay Pottery Studio. Children as young as 5 and as old as 16 or more can learn about basic ceramic techniques, such as hand-building, sculpture, wheelthrowing, decorating, surface treatments, and firings. Some of the techniques in this book have been customized for children. Those with ceramic experience will notice that easy, alternative methods have been developed for things like wedging clay. Also, for safety reasons, certain tools like the needle tool are not used or mentioned in any of the projects.

Each chapter contains detailed project instructions and teaching tips (labelled "Tips for Helpers") that will help you assist your young artist through specific challenges. The projects and chapters are written in order of importance and difficulty. Basic information is covered in chapter 1, while chapters 2, 3, and 4 provide step-by-step instructions for building projects with wet clay. The children learn about a specific ceramic technique or skill, but they are encouraged to create whatever project they want. A "possible projects board" at the Kids 'N' Clay studio is designed to trigger ideas without telling the children what to make. This same "possible projects" concept will be used throughout the book. You'll notice that each new project becomes more complex as it builds upon previously learned skills.

All the project instructions will direct your child to chapter 5, where they'll learn about a variety of decorating techniques, surface treatments, and firings that will complete the project. Then, finally in "Cracked & Broken Pieces," they'll be introduced to the reality of broken pots and dealing with loss and change. Your child will learn how to think through their options when something breaks. Sometimes things don't work out exactly the way they were planned.

The last section in the book is the "Glossary of Ceramic Terms." This handy reference guide will help your child understand some of those special ceramic words that are used throughout the book.

Purchasing Supplies & Services

Overall, you will find that ceramics is a relatively inexpensive art medium. The handful of tools, underglazes, and glazes that you need to purchase are similar in price to buying cooking utensils; and a 25 pound bag of clay probably costs less than a pad of large drawing paper. In our area of Northern California, basic getting-started costs would be less than $40. (See supply list in chapter 1, page 3.) Once your child's project is built and dried, you'll need to plan for firing costs. Most places charge for the space that a project takes up in the kiln. Prices will vary from location to location, but they are generally reasonable.

When purchasing low-fire clay from a supplier, please use the following description to ensure that you get the right clay body. Tell the supplier that you need a smooth, low-fire clay that has a cone of 06 to 04. (Cone refers to the temperature at which clay become ceramic.) Please note: Red clay is another option, but it stains both clothes and hands.

Also, only ask for low-fire, nontoxic underglazes and glazes. These contain no lead, which means projects will be safe for eating and drinking after the glaze firing is complete (see chapter 5, pages 104 to 109, for more details about underglazing and glazing).

For safety reasons, all clay, underglaze, and low-fire glaze product descriptions or labels should read, "certified nontoxic, conforms to ASTM C-1023/D-4236." The American Society for Testing and Materials (ASTM) Committee on Standards sets standards for hazardous material labeling on art materials.

The materials recommended in this book are considered nontoxic and nonhazardous by today's standards to the best of our knowledge. Because potentially hazardous substances are available for the adult market, anyone using this book should use their best judgement and common sense when selecting supplies. The authors, illustrator, and publisher shall not be liable in any event for incidental or consequential damages in connection with, or arising out of the furnishing, performance, or use of the procedures and techniques herein.

Finding a Local Supplier

There are several ways to find the closest ceramic retailer or supplier in your area. First, look in your local phone book in the yellow pages under the following areas:

★ Ceramic Equipment & Supplies–Retail

★ Ceramic Instruction/Lab Time

★ Art Supplies–Retail

★ Art College/University Bookstores

Second, if you have access to a computer and the Internet, you can do a keyword search online. You can research local retail suppliers and contact them directly, or make remote purchases online from suppliers in other parts of the country. Keyword searches can be done through search engines like Yahoo, InfoSeek, LYCOS, etc. You can also search through online yellow page directories that limit your search to a specific city and state. Here are some keywords to help you with your search:

★ Ceramic

★ Ceramic Equipment & Supplies

★ Ceramic–Domestic Studios Supplies

★ Arts & Crafts

★ Artists Materials & Supplies

★ Low-Fire Clay

You can also reference the Kids 'N' Clay web site at www.kidsnclay.com for additional information on ceramic supplies and resources.

Finally, you can contact organized groups or associations that have formalized ceramic programs. Just ask if you can purchase clay and supplies from them directly. You might even want to take a class or sign up for open studio time.

Firing Finished Work

Because the firing process requires a trained technician who can raise and lower the heat levels in the kiln to the necessary temperatures, you will also need to find a place that can fire your child's finished work when their project is complete. Some ceramic suppliers also fire completed projects. Those who don't can probably refer you to a local, reputable business that does.

So, are you ready to get started? Put on your cheerleading hat and let's begin with chapter 1!

1

Welcome to the Studio

• •

Children at the Kids 'N' Clay Pottery Studio working on handbuilding, sculpture, and wheel-thrown projects.

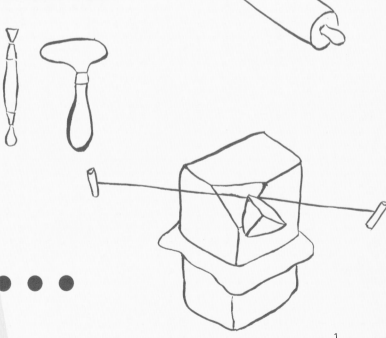

WELCOME TO THE STUDIO

There is an artist who needs nurturing within each child.
—Kevin Nierman

You Can Make Anything with Clay

Just imagine all the wonderful ceramic projects you can make for yourself, your family, and your friends. You won't be using colored molding clay, baker's dough, or Play-Doh. You'll be working with the same materials that professional ceramic artists use. Once you get started, you'll see just how fun ceramics can be. No experience is needed, because your adult helper is there to guide you. Just follow the steps and you'll be surprised at what you can do. When your project is finished, it may not look like the pictures in this book. These are only examples of what others have done. Make your project look the way that *you* want.

THINKING CREATIVELY

Let's begin by preparing your brain for some creative thinking. Try to remember these positive messages before beginning every project:

★ **Be Open...** Welcome and consider new things and new ideas.

★ **Explore More...** Experiment and try new things with clay.

★ **Imagine...** Make believe that anything is possible.

★ **Enjoy Creating...** Have fun making things in clay, even if you don't keep your project in the end.

★ **Think Safety...** Be careful with your tools and equipment so that no one gets hurt.

★ **Clean Up Before You Leave...** Be considerate of yourself and others by leaving a clean area and clean tools for your next use.

Studio Tips for Helpers

This section is designed to welcome and familiarize your child with the ceramic tools and materials that they will be using. You can purchase all your materials and supplies at once using the master list in this chapter, or you can build up your studio supplies slowly by using the "You Will Need" list before each project. In either case, the illustrations and descriptions in this section will help you identify the tools and equipment that your child will need for the projects in this book.

Setting Up Your Studio

Before you start a project, you'll need to prepare your ceramic studio. Think of your studio as your special workshop where you can make ceramic masterpieces without being disturbed. This is where you'll have all the supplies and tools that you need. Your studio can be in your kitchen, the garage, the backyard, or a classroom. Here's a list of important things you will need in your studio. You will probably find some of these tools and supplies in your kitchen, but you'll need to buy a few new things too. If you like to keep organized, a plastic toolbox or container is a great way to store all your tools.

Studio Materials & Supplies

■ **A Comfortable Place to Work:** A nice big worktable and a chair will do. If you like, you can work on the floor too!

■ **Wooden Board Covered with Canvas:** You'll need to build all your projects on this portable, nonstick work surface. The size of

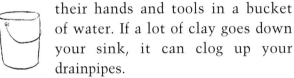

the board really depends on the size of your project, but 2 feet by 2 feet or 2 feet by 4 feet is a good size for most projects in this book. You can buy the canvas at an art supply or a fabric store. You will need to attach this to the underside of the board with tacks or staples from a staple gun to prevent it from slipping.

■ **Storage Shelves:** These are optional. You just need a safe place to store your projects where they won't get bumped or knocked over.

■ **Big Bucket of Water:** This is optional, but recommended. Many ceramic artists clean their hands and tools in a bucket of water. If a lot of clay goes down your sink, it can clog up your drainpipes.

■ **Electric Potter's Wheel:** This is optional and for wheel-throwing projects only. You can purchase a potter's wheel from a ceramic supplier, or you can take an open studio class at a school or studio that already has one.  Kick wheels are also available but are not recommended for children who are learning to throw.

■ **White Low-Fire Clay:** This light-colored clay does not stain clothes. It's usually available in a 25-pound bag or 50-pound box for a very reasonable price. Red clay is also available, but it does stain clothes and hands.

Cut-Off Tool: This handy tool is used to cut off big chunks of clay. For safety reasons, make sure that you get a cut-off tool made of string rather than wire.

Small Sponges: These are important for keeping your clay moist or for smoothing the surface of your clay, especially if you are wheel-throwing.

Bowl of Water: You'll want to keep this close by for wetting your hands and rinsing your sponges.

Wooden Tool: This is used to make designs in your project.

Fork: A kitchen fork works well for scoring clay.

Slip or Slushy Clay: Slip is liquid clay and acts like glue. It's actually just a mixture of clay and water. You can make it yourself by putting a few small pieces of clay in a jar with some water. Shake it up until it is the consistency of mustard. If you put your slip in a plastic squeeze bottle, it's easy to use and store. No refrigeration is required.

Rolling Pin: Ask if you can borrow one from the kitchen, or get your own just for rolling clay.

Wooden Boards: These thin pieces of wooden trim ($1/4$ to $1/2$ inch thick, 1 to 2 inches wide, about 2 feet long) are used to keep clay even when you are rolling out your clay with a rolling pin.

Plastic-Coated Paper Clip: When you straighten out one end of the paper clip, it becomes a handy poking tool. Use it to make holes in hollow projects or to check the bottom thickness of your pots.

Ruler or Straightedge: You'll need this handy tool when you cut out straight lines or edges. The ruler is important for measuring the thickness of your clay too.

Butter Knife or Fettling Knife: These are great for cutting and slicing clay. You should use a knife with a rounded tip, not a pointed one.

Small Boards: These wooden or plastic boards will be used to store your projects between building stages until they are bisque-fired.

Plastic Wrap or Dry-Cleaning Bags: Wrapping your project in plastic will prevent it from drying out when you take a break.

Spray Bottle: You can lightly spray water on your project before wrapping it in plastic. A spray bottle is also helpful when you need to wet your clay for recycling.

Newspaper: Crumpled newspaper can be used as a mold to give your clay more shape when you are making sculptures. See chapter 3 for more details. You'll also want to cover your underglazing and low-fire glazing area with  newspaper so drips and spills can be quickly cleaned up.

- **Bat:** For wheel-throwing projects only. This is the round board that goes over the potter's wheel. It allows you to remove your project from the wheel without touching it.

- **Trimming Tool:** For wheel-throwing projects only. This tool helps you remove excess clay on wheel-thrown projects. See chapter 4, page 83 for more details.

- **Underglazes:** Nontoxic underglazes are applied on clay before it is fired. It provides both color and detailed design options for the first firing. This can be painted on the surface of your project.

- **Low-Fire Glazes:** Nontoxic, low-fire glazes are applied to *bisque-fired* projects that have already been fired in the kiln once. Glazes are typically used to seal the surface with a glassy protective coating. This may be a color glaze or a clear glaze. You can paint or dip these coatings on your projects.

- **Small Bucket:** You'll pour your low-fire glaze into a small bucket when dip glazing your projects.

- **Dipping Tongs:** If you don't want to get your hands messy while dip glazing, dipping tongs will keep your hands away from the glazes.

- **Paintbrushes:** When you paint on your underglaze or glaze, you should have small brushes for detailing and larger brushes for covering open areas.

- **Plastic Tool Box or Container:** This will keep all your tools organized in one place.

- **Carrying Box:** You should have a special carrying box to protect your work when you move it to and from the kiln. A cardboard filing box works great because of the carrying handles. By padding the inside of the box with soft cloth, towels, or newspaper, you can add more protection.

- **Reference Materials:** Having materials for reference in your studio is like having your own mini-library of visual ideas. It's helpful to have books and magazines around whether you want to make a ceramic car or a tiger sculpture. Then, you can see the shape of the car hood or exactly how far back the tiger's ears go on its head. Here are some reference ideas. You'll probably come up with a few more on your own.

National Geographic
Travel, animal, or car magazines
Favorite photos or postcards
Picture books
Stamps and stickers

Understanding the Ceramic Process

Here is a brief overview of the four stages that you will go through with each project. As you begin building your projects, you will see the importance of controlling how fast the clay dries. You'll also discover what you can and can't do at each stage.

STAGE 1: BUILDING WITH WET CLAY

New clay—right out of the bag—is soft, moist, and ready to use. You can make it into many different shapes and forms. Just remember to keep your clay moist when you are working on your project. It's also wise to keep a bowl of water close by. Once your clay begins to dry, you won't be able to change its shape. You'll also notice that clay shrinks slightly as it dries. You'll want to build your project a little bigger than you want it to be when it's finished. Note: How quickly or slowly clay dries depends heavily on the weather.

STAGE 2: DETAILING WITH LEATHER-HARD CLAY

After you've formed the final shape of your project, let it air-dry for about a day. You'll see how the clay stiffens and the project begins to hold its shape. It becomes what is called "leather-hard." At this point, you can carve it, polish it, poke air holes in it, or decorate it. You can also attach small clay objects or handles. It's still slightly damp, so you can add detail without breaking it, but you won't be able to change its overall shape.

STAGE 3: DECORATING ON BONE-DRY CLAY

When your project is decorated and all your finishing touches are complete, you'll want to let your leather-hard project air-dry for at least three days. When it's completely dry and no moisture is left, it's called "bone-dry." You'll notice a color change at this stage. White clay will go from the darker grayish brown, leather-hard stage to the chalky white, bone-dry stage. Red clay will go from a dark brick red to a chalky reddish brown color that looks like an eraser on a pencil. At this point the clay cannot be carved or changed, but your project is still very fragile. Many people like to add underglaze colors to their bone-dry projects before they get fired. (See chapter 5, page 104, for more information on underglazing.)

STAGE 4: FIRING IN THE KILN

You'll want to take your project to a place where it can be fired in a kiln. A kiln is a special furnace or clay oven that is designed to safely increase the temperature from 0°F to 1944°F over several hours, so the final transformation can take place. This temperature is much hotter than in a kitchen oven, which only reaches temperatures up to 450°F to 500°F. When exposed to the proper heat levels, the clay changes from a fragile state to a hard, durable form that becomes ceramic. A ceramic lab worker will control the heat levels in the kiln to lessen the risk of a project breaking.

If water or air is trapped inside your clay, the pressure from the steam may cause your project to crack or break in the kiln. That's why your project must be completely bone-dry before it is fired. Also, if you have an enclosed hollow project, you'll need to make air holes somewhere, so the steam can escape. (It's best to make air holes at the leather-hard stage.)

Your project will probably be fired twice. It will be bisque-fired the first time with or without underglazes, which are applied before the firing to add color. The second firing can be a glaze firing, which adds a waterproof protective coating when the glaze melts, or a smoke firing, which is for decorative projects only.

Please note: Glaze-fired projects are safe for food and drinks, but should only be washed by hand. We do not recommend putting these in the dishwasher or the microwave. Low-fire glazes tend to chip in the dishwasher, and some glazes will form a pattern of small cracks when heated in the microwave. If you decide to smoke-fire your project without glazes, it will not be safe for eating or drinking.

Getting to Know Clay

Do you know where clay comes from? Clay is a natural product that is developed by the earth. It's made of decomposed rock that has been broken down by rain, snow, frost, and wind over millions of years. You can find clay deposits by digging into fertile areas of the earth. In the past, people would use the clay just as they found it in the earth. Today, various materials and minerals are added to the clay to create different kinds of ceramic pottery. You just buy your clay from a local ceramic supply store and it's ready to use. There's no digging!

Warm-Up Tips for Helpers

Getting your child comfortable with touching clay and experiencing how it behaves is the purpose of this section. Together, you can practice some of the basic steps that will be used in many of the projects ahead. This is also a great opportunity to just play and experiment, without worrying about a project.

The Basics

The best way to learn about clay is to play with it. So gather some clay and your tools, and let's go over some basic steps:

1) CUTTING NEW CLAY:

When you first buy your clay, it's ready to use right out of the bag. Just cut off the amount of clay that you need with your cut-off tool.

■ Pull both handles outward so that the string is tight and straight.

■ Place the cut-off tool behind the clay that you want to cut away.

■ Then, pull toward you to slice off a chunk of clay. It works like a giant cheese cutter.

2) ATTACHING PIECES:

Scoring is how two pieces of clay are joined together. You will use these steps to attach a cup handle or two walls that form the corner of a box.

- Use a fork to scratch the two places that will be attached.

- Put slip on the places you just scratched. You can squeeze out some slip from a plastic bottle or paint some on with a paint brush.

- Then firmly press the two pieces together and seal the edges by smoothing the clay around the crease until the line is gone.

3) WATERING YOUR CLAY:

Exposure to air will slowly dry out the clay, and your project can become too hard to work with. If you see tiny cracks in the clay or your clay becomes stiff, these are the first signs that your clay is getting thirsty.

- Wet your fingers and rub water in the cracked areas until the clay is smooth.

- Using too much water can dissolve the clay into a mushy slip, so add water slowly.

- Also, make sure that your bag of unused clay is sealed airtight, so it won't dry out.

- If the clay you are working with is getting too stiff, cut it into small pieces and try recycling it (see the next step).

4) RECYCLING & REMOVING AIR BUBBLES:

After you've worked on a few projects, you may have a pile of scrap or used clay that is building up. As long as the clay is still moist, it can be recycled and used on a new project. Recycling is a method of combining two or more pieces of clay so that they act like one piece of clay. This process is called "wedging." You want to make sure there is no trapped air inside the clay. This is especially important if you are working on the potter's wheel.

- First, squish all the clay pieces together. The clay should be almost as moist as new clay. Sometimes a little water needs to be added. Drip some water on the clay with your hands, or use a spray bottle to wet the clay.

- Next, form a clay ball.

■ Then, throw the clay ball down on the canvas-covered board as hard as you can. Repeat this step about 20 times, turning the clay ball slightly so a different side hits the table each time.

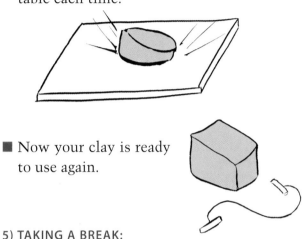

■ Now your clay is ready to use again.

5) TAKING A BREAK:

If you need to stop working in the middle of your project, make sure that you cover it with plastic completely. Remember, once your clay dries, you cannot change its shape.

Dry-cleaning bags are great, and plastic wrap works well too. Just make sure that you tuck and wrap the plastic closely against your project so no air can reach your work. A damp paper towel under the plastic can help keep the clay moist too if you need to leave your project for more than a few days.

6) LEAVING YOUR MARK:

Every artist has a special way of signing their work, so don't forget to identify all your projects. That way, people will know that you were the artist. It's also nice to add the date so you know when you made it.

Use a pencil or a plastic-coated paper clip to scratch into the bottom of your project after it becomes leather-hard. You can write your name, your initials, the date, or your own special mark.

7) STORING & DRYING:

When you are not working on your project, you need to find a place to store it where no one will bother it. (That includes pets!) This is where all your projects will be kept when you are taking a break, when you are drying a project, and when your project is waiting to be fired in the kiln. Maybe you have room in your studio, or maybe there's a spot in your bedroom closet.

Now that you've learned the basic steps, let's move on to chapter 2 so you can make your first handbuilding project.

Handbuilding Projects

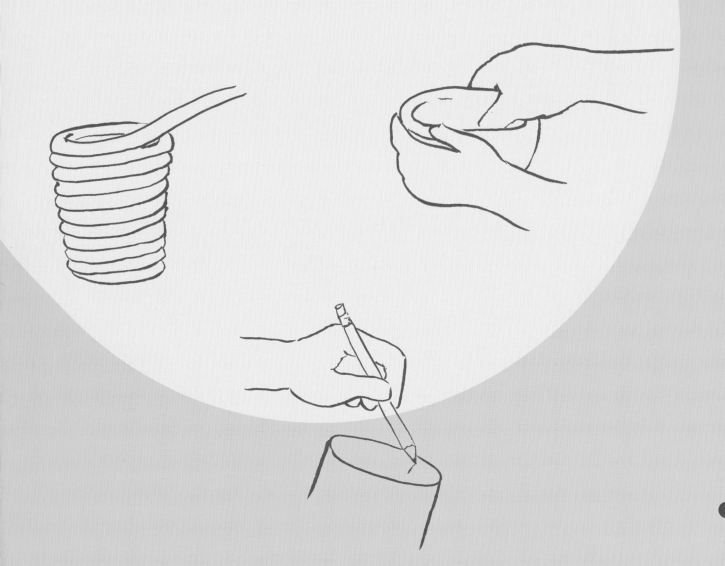

Lea carefully attaches gingerbread man cutouts to the rim of a huge bowl that she made by pressing a clay slab into a mold.

HANDBUILDING PROJECTS

··

With clay, you can actually create things that don't exist—
like an arm with Mt. Everest on one side.
—Courtney

What Is Handbuilding?

Handbuilding is a general term used to describe the way pottery and ceramic sculptures are made by hand rather than on a potter's wheel. This chapter will introduce you to three of the most popular handbuilding methods—pinch, coil, and slab. You'll also find the steps for building more than 14 fun projects. Once you are familiar with these basic handbuilding skills, you can make hundreds of projects on your own!

This chapter only covers the first stage of the ceramic process. When you are done building with wet clay, please go to chapter 5 to learn about adding designs in clay, decorating with underglazes and glazes, and firing ceramics.

These are a few things you should do before working with clay. First, read chapter 1 before beginning a project. Next, gather all the tools and supplies you need for your project. It's important to be prepared before you start. Then, decide what you'd like to make before you begin. You can work from the list of possible projects or from your own ideas.

I like working with clay because you get to build what you want. If you find a cardboard box,
you can't mold it into just anything.
—Hayden

Pinch Pots & More!

Pinch pots are a great way to get to know clay. These projects are both fun and useful. They're also not very big because they are first formed in the palm of your hand. Your thumb and your forefinger are the most important tools for pinch projects.

Pinch Project Tips for Helpers

If this is your child's first project in clay, you might want to make your own pinch pot, so you can demonstrate each step along the way. As you troubleshoot any problems, younger children (ages five to seven) may want you to fix their problems rather than tell them what to do. Learning by example can be very valuable to children as long as you explain each step as you are doing it. We recommend that you begin with "The Original Pinch Pot" project, so you can help build your child's comfort and confidence with clay. Then, your young artist can decide what their next project will be on their own. After you've completed the basic project steps in this chapter, move forward to chapter 5 to learn about decorating and surface treatments.

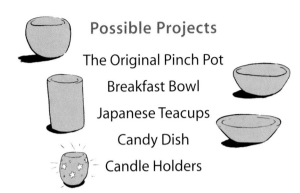

Possible Projects

The Original Pinch Pot

Breakfast Bowl

Japanese Teacups

Candy Dish

Candle Holders

You Will Need:

- canvas-covered board to work on

- white low-fire clay

- cut-off tool to cut clay

- bowl of water to wet your hands

- large plastic-coated paper clip to check thickness of bottom or write your name

- ruler to measure thickness of clay

- butter knife or fettling knife to cut clay

- pencil to write your name or create designs (optional)

- plastic wrap or dry-cleaning bags to prevent your project from drying (optional)

- spray bottle of water (optional)

THE ORIGINAL PINCH POT

This pot can be used for anything from holding paper clips to planting flowers. It's easy to make too!

Pinch Pot by Emily

1 With your cut-off tool, cut a piece of clay about the size of your fist.

Roll the clay into a ball.

2 Push your thumb into the center of the ball. Stop when you are about $1/2$ inch from the bottom.

3 To check the thickness of the bottom, straighten the end of your plastic-coated paper clip and use it to push through the bottom of your clay. Note where it hits the bottom, and meaure it with a ruler.

Q: Oops, my thumb went through my project!

A: Don't worry. Just push the clay back in place and patch the hole with a small flattened piece of clay. Then, smooth the patched area by rubbing the clay with some water.

4 Now pinch the clay between your thumb and your fingers and begin rotating the pot in the palm of your hand. Watch how the walls of your Pinch Pot begin to grow as it gets thinner.

5 Place your Pinch Pot on your canvas-covered board when it gets too big for your hand. This will flatten the bottom of your pot. When the walls are as thin and tall as you want (between $1/2$ and $1/4$ inch thick), your project will be finished.

6 Use a pencil to write your name in your clay. Now you can decorate or dry your project.

BREAKFAST BOWL

Wouldn't it be fun to eat your morning cereal from a special breakfast bowl that was made and designed by you? You could use it for a giant ice cream sundae on special occasions too.

Breakfast Bowl by Mitchell

1. Follow steps 1 to 4 for an Original Pinch Pot on pages 14 and 15.

2. You can change the shape of your pinch pot by gently rubbing and pressing the clay in or out. To make a bowl, pinch the clay a little thinner and gently press out to make the top wider.

3. You can also add more clay to make a bigger bowl. Simply pinch in small pieces of new clay. Keep turning your project as you add clay so that the thickness is even on all sides.

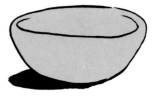

4. Use a pencil to write your name in your clay. You are now ready to decorate or dry your project.

JAPANESE TEACUPS

These traditional teacups are easy to make because they don't have handles. In Japan, tea ceremonies are held to show friendship and trust. You can make enough cups to share with all your close friends and family. Then you can have your own tea party.

Japanese Teacups by Madeleine

1 Start with a small ball of clay, about the size of an egg. Then follow steps 1 to 4 for an Original Pinch Pot on pages 14 and 15.

2 Make the bottom of your teacup about 2 inches across.

|— 2" —|

3 The side walls can be as high as you like. A nice size for drinking tea is 3 inches or taller.

4 Use a pencil to write your name in your clay. Now you can decorate or dry your project.

CANDY DISH

What will your candy dish hold—chocolate-covered raisins, Kisses, lemon drops, or maybe jelly beans? Making a candy dish is like making a bowl except the bottom is wider and the walls are shorter. This will give you more space to hold your sweet treats.

Candy Dish by Jacob

1   Follow steps 1 to 4 for the Original Pinch Pot on pages 14 and 15, but use a ball of clay the size of a grapefruit. After pushing your thumb in the center of the clay ball, pinch out the bottom base until it's at least 4 inches across.

2   Then, build up the sides as high as you like and gently press the walls out to make a bowl. (About 2 or 3 inches is a good height.)

3   Use a pencil to write your name in your clay. Now you can decorate or dry your project.

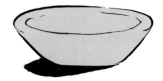

CANDLE HOLDERS

Candle holders are great gifts, especially for the holidays. The candlelight will shine through the spaces that you cut away. Try pinching in different designs, drawing into the clay with a pencil, or adding pieces of clay to make an animal face.

Candle Holder by Ryan

1 Follow steps 1 to 4 for the Original Pinch Pot on pages 14 and 15, but make sure your base is at least 3 inches across. You'll need enough space for a small candle to fit inside.

2 You'll want to pinch in extra clay to build your side walls. The walls should be at least 4 inches high. You can make your walls straight or curve them in or out.

3 If you want to add designs, you should do it while your clay is still soft.

TURN THE PAGE →

4   Next, let your project dry overnight.

5   Once your project becomes leather-hard, very carefully use your fettling knife to cut out small pieces of the clay wall on all sides. This can be done in a pattern, or you can cut out shapes to make a face, an animal, or lots of little stars.

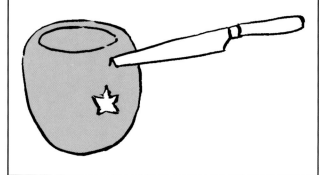

Tip: Make sure that you don't cut away too much of the clay, or your side walls will become too weak. You should have at least $1/2$ inch between each piece that you cut away.

6   Use a pencil to write your name in your clay. Now you can decorate or dry your project.

Snake Cups & Other Stuff

You will be building the next five projects with long rolls of clay that look like snakes. This is known as the "coil method." You can create flat designs or stack your coils on top of each other to form taller shapes. There are two secrets to a good coil project: learning how to roll a snake coil, and keeping your coils very close together.

Coil Project Tips for Helpers

Kids really enjoy working with coils because they can build tall projects. Learning to roll an even coil and keeping coils closely joined together are the challenges. Once the coils are stacked, you will be helping your child smooth and blend the coils together. Spaces between coils may cause cracks when the project dries. Trapped air in the space may also cause problems in the kiln.

The problems and tips outlined in the Pinch Pot section (pages 13 to 20) also apply to coil projects.

Possible Projects

 Cool Coasters

 Snake Cup

 Soup Bowl

 Snacking Plate

 Swinging Bell

You Will Need:

- canvas-covered board to work on
- white low-fire clay
- cut-off tool to cut clay
- ruler to measure thickness of clay
- bowl of water to wet your hands
- butter knife or fettling knife to cut clay
- fork to score the clay
- slip to attach pieces together
- medium paintbrush (or plastic squeeze bottle) to apply slip
- sponge to smooth edge of your project
- plastic-coated paper clip to make holes in clay (for swinging bell only)
- string to attach ringer and make handle (for swinging bell only)
- pencil to write your name or create designs (optional)
- spray bottle of water to wet your clay (optional)
- plastic wrap or dry-cleaning bags to keep your project from drying (optional)

HOW TO MAKE A SNAKE COIL

1 Begin by using your cut-off tool to cut off a small piece of clay about the size of your fist.

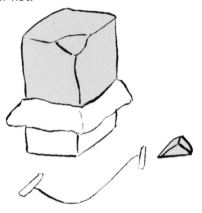

2 Form the clay into an oval or oblong shape with your hands.

3 Use both hands to roll out a long clay snake. Open your fingers wide and roll lightly.

4 Roll a coil as long as you can. It should be about $^1/_2$ inch thick.

Q: Something's wrong. My snake coil won't roll anymore.

A: If you press too hard when you are rolling, the coil can flatten on one side. When this happens, position your coil so that the flat side is not against the table. By using small, short strokes to press down on the top edge, you can make your coil round again.

COOL COASTERS

These Cool Coasters will add some cheer to any room. They make great gifts for different seasons and holidays, or you can make up designs for mom, dad, or your favorite teacher. Once you have finished one, you can make more to create a set.

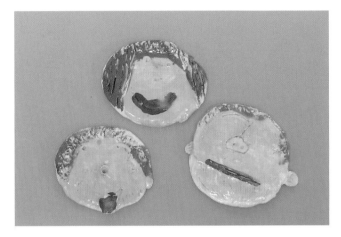

Face Coasters by Melia

1 Roll out as long a coil as you can.

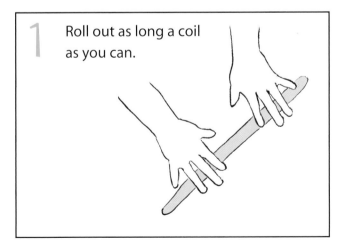

2 Spiral the clay into a tight circle. All the coils should be touching with no spaces in between.

3 This will be the size of your coaster, unless you want to add another coil to make it bigger. To do this, just place your new coil right where the last one left off and keep winding.

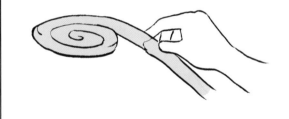

TURN THE PAGE

4 If your coil is too long, just use your butter knife to cut off the part that you don't need.

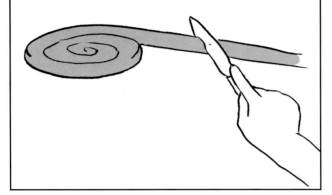

6 Use a pencil to write your name in your clay. Now you can decorate or dry your project.

5 Once the circle is the size you want, smooth and seal all the cracks with your thumb. If you like the spiral design, just smooth one side and leave the spiral coils showing on top.

If you keep the coils showing, this project looks kind of like a snake wrapped around itself. Building the base of the project is the first step. Then you'll build up your side walls. For good support, the base coils should be about 3/4 inch thick, which is a bit thicker than the 1/2 inch-thick side coils.

Snake Cup by Mattison

1 To make the base of your cup, follow the instructions for Cool Coasters on pages 23 and 24. You can make the base as big or small as you like. Anywhere from 3 to 6 inches is a good size. Just make sure that you seal both sides, so you won't have any leaks in your cup!

2 Roll a new coil about 1/2 inch thick. You'll want the coil to go around the base one time. If it's not long enough, add on another coil. This new base layer will be the beginning of your side wall.

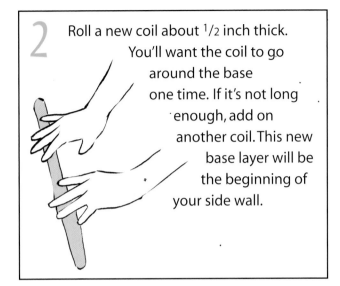

3 Score the bottom of this coil where it will touch the base and then apply slip. Only this first layer needs to be scored.

TURN THE PAGE

4   Also score and apply slip to the rim around the top of the base where the coil will be added.

Tip: If this is your first time scoring clay, see "Attaching Pieces" on page 8 for more details.

5   Attach the first coil to the base by putting the scored and slipped parts together.

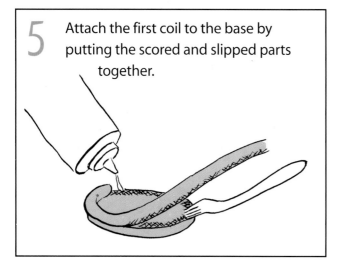

6   Continue rolling and stacking coils until your cup is as tall as you like.

7   Now you need to smooth and seal the cracks on the inside to make it water-tight. You can leave the coils showing on the outside for a design, or you can seal them for a smooth look.

Tip: When sealing and smoothing your side walls, be careful not to push too hard or your walls may get too thin. The shape can also get lopsided. You can prevent this by supporting the opposite side of the wall with one hand when rubbing and smoothing the clay with the other hand.

8 Next, make the handle. Roll another ¹/₂-inch snake coil and flatten it slightly by pressing it down on the table. You can also wet your middle finger and thumb to make a slight dent that runs the whole length of the handle.

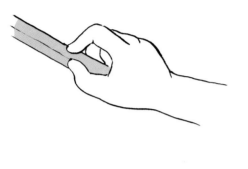

9 Bend it into the shape you want.

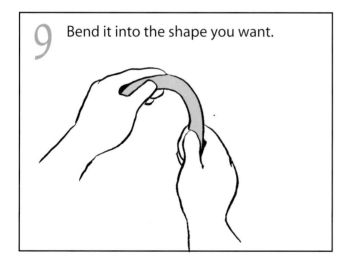

10 Then score and apply slip to the ends of the handle and the places on the cup where they will attach. Press and smooth the handle in place.

Tip: Be careful when you are attaching a handle. You need to support the inside of the cup wall with your hand, so your project will not get pushed out of shape.

11 Use a pencil to write your name in your clay. Now you can decorate or dry your project.

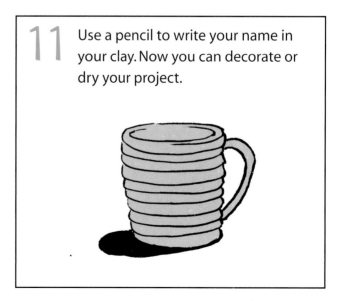

SOUP BOWL

This soup bowl has handles on both sides. Building this project is similar to making Snake Cups, but you'll learn how make the side walls curve in and out.

Soup Bowl by Evan

1 Follow steps 1 to 6 for Snake Cups on pages 25 and 26. (You'll start by making a Cool Coaster as a base.) This time you'll want to stack your coils slightly to the outside edge of the first wall coil to make your bowl wider. Remember to smooth the coils on the inside of your bowl.

2 To make your bowl narrow at the top edge, shift the last few coils slightly to the inside as you stack them on top of each other.
If you want to decorate your soup bowl, smooth the outside coils.

3 To make small handles for both sides, roll two new coils that are each about 3 or 4 inches long.

4 Remember to score and apply slip to the ends of the handles and the places where they will attach. Press and smooth the handles into place.

5 Use a pencil to write your name in your clay. Now you can decorate or dry your project.

SNACKING PLATE

Here's the perfect serving dish for your after-school snacks. You can make designs in the clay or keep the coil design on the surface. Just repeat this project if you want to make a set of dishes to share with all those hungry snackers that you know.

Snacking Plate by Steve

1 Making a coil plate is easy. Follow the instructions for Cool Coasters on pages 23 and 24, but add more coils to make it as big as you want.

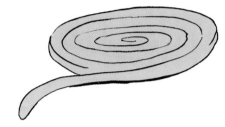

2 Smooth the top of the plate. Then carefully turn it over and smooth the bottom.

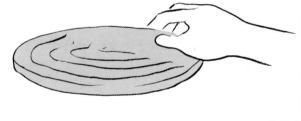

3 Add a coil to the top of the plate to make an edge. You'll want the coil to go around the top of the plate one time. If it's not long enough, add on another coil.

TURN THE PAGE

4 Score the bottom of this coil where it will touch the top of the plate. Then apply slip.

5 To finish the edge, smooth the inside and the outside seam where the new coil touches your plate.

6 Use a pencil to write your name in your clay. Now you can decorate or dry your project.

SWINGING BELL

You can hang this bell outside on the porch or the balcony like a wind chime. You'll hear a ringing sound whenever the wind blows. Any ideas on how to make this project? A bell is basically an upside down cup without the

handles. After everything has been glaze-fired, you will tie a long piece of string through the ringer and the bell. The string becomes a handle.

Swinging Bell by Jessica

1 Just follow steps 1 to 7 for Snake Cups on pages 25 and 26. (You'll start by making a Cool Coaster as the top of the bell.) This time don't add any handles.

2 After you have smoothed the inside (outside is optional), make a small hole in the center of the base. This is where the string will be added later.

3 For the ringer, make a small ball of clay and use your plastic-coated paper clip to make a hole through the middle—like a bead.

4 Use a pencil to write your name in your clay. Now you can decorate or dry your project.

Tip: When you attach the string later, tie a knot on both sides of the bead and the bell so they will stay in place.

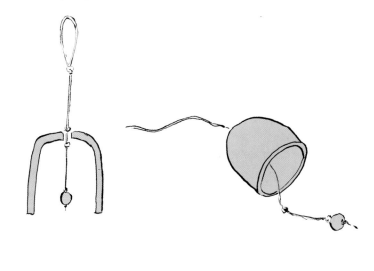

Rolling Pin Creations

Slab projects are also known as rolling pin creations because you form them from flat pieces of clay that are rolled out like cookie dough. First you'll see how slabs are made, then you can make your projects.

Slab Project Tips for Helpers

Slab projects tend to be bigger than pinch and coil projects and may require more hands-on assistance. A good rolling pin and a nonstick work surface are especially important when rolling slabs. Most slabs are rolled to about $1/2$ inch thick. For large projects, the base or side walls may need to be thicker ($3/4$ inch) to support the weight of the project as it grows.

Possible Projects

Hand, Foot, & Paw Prints

Storytelling Bookends

Molds for Bowls

A Bubble Vase

Safety Tip for Helper

Never leave a child alone with the rolling pin. It can roll on the floor and hit their foot, or if misused, can be very dangerous. The rolling pin should not be lifted higher than a child's shoulders.

You Will Need:

- canvas-covered board to work on
- white low-fire clay
- cut-off tool to cut clay
- rolling pin to roll out clay slabs
- wooden boards, $1/2$ inch thick (optional) guides to keep your slab even when rolling your clay
- ruler to measure thickness of clay
- pencil to make a hole in the hot plate or to write your name or a message
- butter knife or fettling knife to cut clay
- bowl of water to wet hands
- fork to score clay
- slip to attach pieces together
- medium paintbrush (or plastic squeeze bottle) to apply slip
- sponge to smooth edge of your project
- spray bottle of water to wet your clay (optional)
- plastic wrap or dry-cleaning bags to keep your project from drying (optional)
- adhesive felt (for hot plate)
- string (for hanging ornament)

HOW TO MAKE A SLAB

1 Begin by cutting off a large piece of clay, about the size of a brick, with your cut-off tool.

2 Use your rolling pin to pound it into a flat shape. It's easier to flatten the clay if you are standing up. Always use both handles on the rolling pin for better strength and safety. You should not lift it any higher than your shoulders.

3 Now begin to roll the clay evenly with your rolling pin. Stop rolling when the clay is about 1/2 inch thick.

4 To help the slab form evenly as you roll it out, you can use wooden boards on each side of the clay as a guide. This helps you get the proper thickness too.

5 This flat piece of clay is called a "slab."

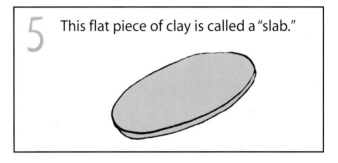

Q: I didn't use wooden boards and my slab has thick and thin spots. How can I fix it?

A: Press harder on the thicker areas to thin them out. Never fold the clay over to make an area thicker. This can form air bubbles, which will cause breaking problems later. If your clay is too thin, you'll need to wedge the clay together and roll out a new slab.

HAND, FOOT, & PAW PRINTS

Making hand, foot, and paw imprints in your projects is a great way to give hot plates, plaques, plates, or garden tiles a personal touch. Don't forget to mark the date and your age on the project, so people will know how old you were when you made it. You can include your whole family by making a special set with everyone's hand, foot, or paw print.

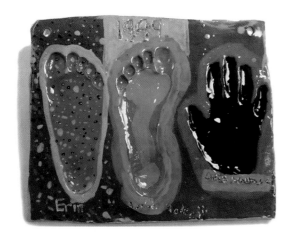

Garden Tile by Erin, Austin, and Luke

1 Roll out a slab about $^1/2$ inch thick.

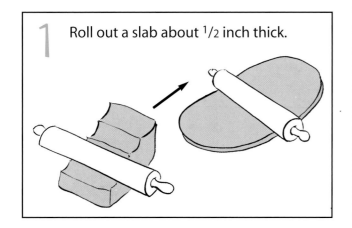

2 Press your hand (or foot or pet's paw) firmly into the clay so it leaves a nice imprint. You can also trace your hand with a pencil if you prefer.

3 Next, write your name, the date, and maybe a personal message in the clay.

4 Now you need to decide what you are going to make. Here are three choices.

To make a hot plate or a garden tile:

After it's been fired in the kiln, a hot plate will need felt protectors on the bottom corners. A garden tile can be placed anywhere you like in the garden. You can start with the hand, foot, or paw imprint you made on page 34.

1 Use your butter knife to cut a square or a circle around the imprint that you just made. In a single motion, slice the clay with your knife. Do not saw because the clay can rip.

2 Use a pencil to write your name in your clay. Now you can decorate or dry your project.

To make a plaque or an ornament:

1 Use your knife to cut around the edges of your imprint, or cut out a square, oval, or circle.

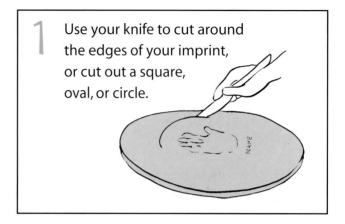

2 Make a hole at the top with your pencil. This is where you can hang it later after it's been fired.

3 Use a pencil to write your name in your clay. Now you can decorate or dry your project.

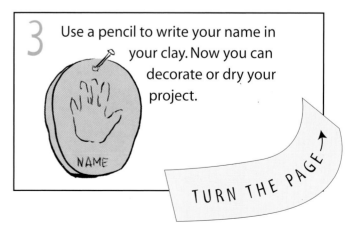

TURN THE PAGE ➜

To make a plate:

1 Use your knife to cut a circle or an oval around your imprint.

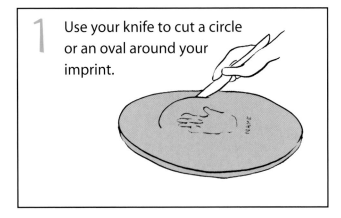

2 Then roll out a coil.

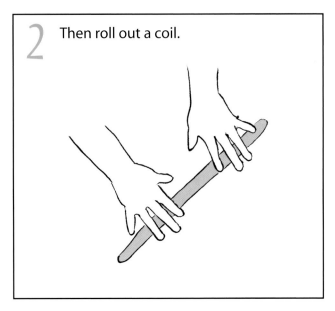

3 Score the coil and the rim of the slab. Apply slip and seal the coil on the edge of the slab.

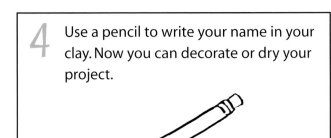

4 Use a pencil to write your name in your clay. Now you can decorate or dry your project.

STORYTELLING BOOKENDS

This project can be as simple or complex as you like. Once the basic bookend form is shaped, you can decorate the bent slabs or build a complete scene or a mini-sculpture on both bookends. Your bookends can be a matching set, or each one can be completely different. It's entirely up to you. Here are a few ideas:

★ Make a little scene from your favorite story.

★ Spell your name in coils surrounded by some of your favorite things (or someone else's favorite things if it's a gift).

★ Show the front side of an animal or person on one bookend, and the back side on the other.

★ Build little gargoyles or angels that sit on each side.

Storytelling Bookends by Roxanne

1 Begin by rolling a slab about 3/4 inch thick. It should be about 14 inches long by 7 inches wide.

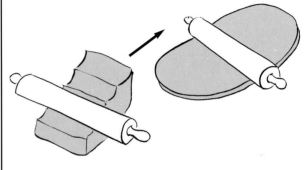

2 Use your ruler to measure and cut out a rectangle that is 12 inches long by 6 inches wide.

TURN THE PAGE

3 Carefully lift up one end of the slab and prop half of it up against a wall or something steady. It should look like an L.

Q: My slab is starting to crack. What should I do?

A: If the crack isn't too deep, smooth it out with a damp sponge. A deeper crack may need some patching and smoothing with a new piece of clay. In general, clay tends to crack when it gets dried out or you work with it too much. Make sure you keep your hands damp and keep your bowl of water close by.

4 Repeat steps 1 to 3 to make the other side of the bookend.

5 Next you can build a scene using the pinch and coil techniques that you learned earlier. You can also add decorations by scoring and applying slip to clay cut outs or clay objects that you wish to attach.

6 Use a pencil to write your name in your clay. Now you can decorate or dry your project.

PRESS MOLDS FOR BOWLS & PLATES

Since a clay slab is soft and flexible, it can take on the shape of other objects when it dries. If you want to make a bowl, find a bowl shape you like and use it as a mold. If you want to make a plate, use a plate you like. Also try glass or metal objects like cake molds and pie pans. You'll need some nonstick cooking spray or plastic wrap to prevent the clay from sticking to your mold. And you'll need to let your clay dry for about a day between steps 7 and 8. If you have some leaves, lace, or rubber stamps around, you can press designs into the clay before you begin molding your project.

Press-Molded Bowl by Arik

You Will Need:

- Leaves, lace, fabric, rubber stamps
- Glass or metal bowls, plates, cake or pie pans
- Nonstick cooking spray or plastic wrap
- Extra clay to add designs (optional)
- Cookie cutters to make additional designs

1 Roll out a slab that is 3/4 inch thick and large enough to cover your mold.

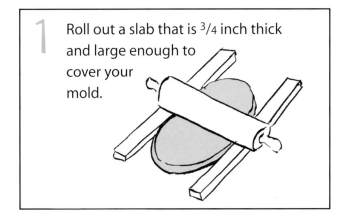

2 (Optional) Now place leaves, lace, or fabric over the clay and roll them into clay with your rolling pin. You can also press them in by hand or make designs with rubber stamps.

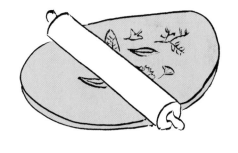

TURN THE PAGE →

3 Lift the lace or fabric off the clay, and a textured design will remain. Leaves can stay in the clay, if you want, because they will burn out in the kiln. Decide if you would like the design on the outside of the bowl (face down), or the inside (face up).

5 Lay your slab over the mold and press the clay down so it touches the mold in all areas.

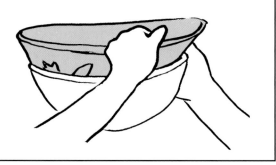

4 When your slab is ready, generously spray your mold with oil or line it with plastic wrap.

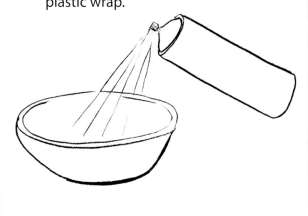

6 Lean your butter knife against the edge of your mold and slice away the extra clay. Try to avoid sawing the clay, or you'll end up with jagged edges.

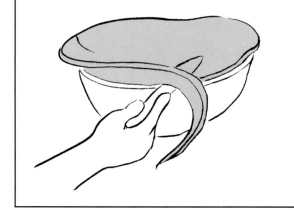

7 Use a damp sponge to smooth the outside edge.

8 When the clay stiffens (in about one day), take it out of the mold and smooth the edges again by rubbing it with a damp sponge.

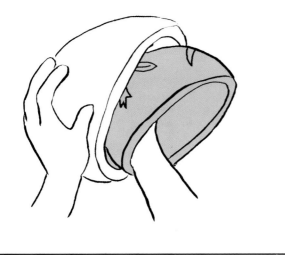

9 For something a little more fancy, you can add spiral coils, little animals, fruit, or vegetables from extra clay scraps.

You can also use a cookie cutter to make new shapes. Just score, apply slip, and seal your designs into place.

10 Use a pencil to write your name in your clay. Now you can decorate or dry your project.

BUBBLE VASE

This round vase is great for holding fresh flowers or dried potpourri. It's made from two press-molded bowls that are the same size.

Bubble Vase by Katie

1 Follow steps 1 to 7 for Press Molds for Bowls & Plates on pages 39 to 41. When the clay stiffens and holds its shape it is leather-hard. (This will take about a day indoors, much less if outside.) Then take it out of the mold and wrap it in plastic.

2 Repeat steps 1 to 7 for Press Molds for Bowl & Plates with a new slab of clay. When the clay stiffens, take it out of the mold.

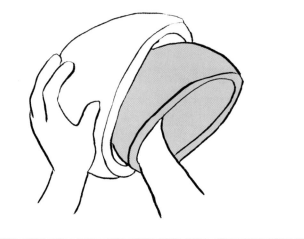

3 Score and apply slip to the edges of both bowls.

4 Roll out a skinny coil.

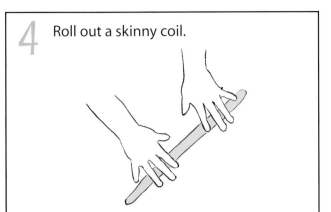

5 Attach the two bowls and seal the seam with the coil. Smooth the coil so it blends in with the body of the vase.

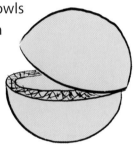

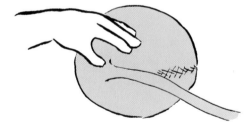

If the two halves don't match up perfectly, just push the clay around so that the edges line up.

6 Now roll out a big thick coil for the base, about 3/4 inch thick. Make a circle with the coil, large enough to support the round vase.

7 Score, apply slip, and attach the coil to the bottom of the vase. This will become your base, or foot.

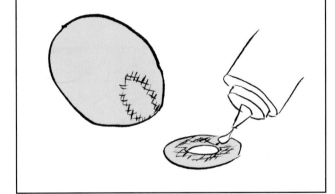

TURN THE PAGE →

8 Cut a hole in the top to make an opening. The hole can be a circle, square, triangle, or even a rectangle. Do whatever you think will work best with your design.

9 Then smooth the edges of the opening with a damp sponge.

Q: There are fingerprints all over my project. How can I get rid of them?

A: Just rub a damp sponge across the surface and they will disappear.

10 Use a pencil to write your name in your clay. Now you can decorate or dry your project.

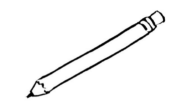

3
Sculptures

Maya uses scraps of foam to support her cat sculpture's head and body as she attaches them together.

SCULPTURES

There's lots of things you can do with clay,
so it's easy to get out what's in your imagination.—Julia

My hands are free when I use clay.—Isaac

Making Sculptures

A sculpture can be a statue, a figure, or any interesting shape. It can be something real like a tree or something from a dream or your imagination. It can be something big or something small—it's all up to you. Sculptures are usually made for looking at, rather than for using. They are often put on display in the living room, on a bookshelf, in a garden, or in a museum. But some sculptures can also be used as doorstops, bookends, or paperweights. In this chapter, you'll combine all the handbuilding skills you've learned in previous chapters to create animal sculptures and interesting art forms with wet clay. Remember, these are just ideas. If you have something special you'd rather make, you can adapt these steps to your own project. Once your project is built, go to chapter 5 to learn about decorating, surface treatments, and firing methods.

Sculpture Tips for Helpers

Your child may not know what a sculpture is, but after you explain that it can be anything at all, they'll have no problem executing their visions. There are a handful of common obstacles that children run into. Most are about supporting the clay, or figuring out how to make a foot or tail look the way they want. It's helpful to keep lots of good reference materials close by. Please note that newspaper, unlike other molding materials, does not need to be removed. It can be fired inside the project and will simply turn into ashes. Nichrome wire is available at most ceramic supply stores. For safety reasons, it is best to insert the wire after all the handbuilding is done to avoid mixing the cut wire in scraps of clay. Only adults should use or have access to the wire cutters.

One of the final steps to many sculpture projects is to poke a couple of holes in hollow closed objects with a straightened plastic-coated paper clip. This will let the trapped steam escape in the kiln and keep your project from cracking or exploding.

Animal Sculptures

Your family will welcome these new pets in the house or the garden. They don't need much food, and they don't make a mess. For this project, you'll be using large slabs of clay with bunched-up newspaper to form the body and head of your animal sculpture. You will also use coil and pinch methods to add the finishing details. The first four animal projects make sitting animals. Standing animals need extra strong legs. You'll learn how to make objects stand in another sculpture project (see page 60).

Possible Projects

Sitting Cat

Floppy-Eared Dog

Mystic Dragon

Hairy Bear

Standing Animal

Prickly Porcupine

You Will Need:

- canvas-covered board to work on

- white low-fire clay

- cut-off tool to cut your clay

- rolling pin to roll out clay slabs

- ruler to measure thickness of clay

- newspaper to crumple and support clay

- bowl of water to wet hands

- butter knife to cut clay

- fork to score clay

- slip to attach pieces

- medium paint brush (or plastic squeeze bottle) to apply slip

- reference materials to give you more ideas

- large plastic-coated paper clip to check thickness of bottom

- plastic wrap or dry-cleaning bags to prevent your project from drying (optional)

- 28-gauge Nichrome wire (optional, for cat and porcupine only)

- wire cutters for cutting wire (optional, for cat and porcupine only)

You'll see how this friendly cat can be easily changed into other sitting animals that are shown in this chapter. Check them all out and then decide which one you'd like to make.

Sitting Cat by Meaghan

1 Begin by cutting off a large piece of clay with your cut-off tool. It should be about the size of a brick.

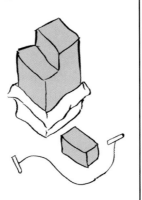

2 Roll the clay into a slab about 3/4 inch thick. It will be used to form the main body of your animal.

3 Get a single sheet of newspaper and bunch it up. Place it on top of the clay slab.

4 Add several more sheets of bunched-up newspaper until you've formed the general shape of the body—in this case, the body of a cat.

5 Now you are going to mold the slab tightly around the newspaper. It's kind of like wrapping a present. First, pull the long sides of the slab up and over the newspaper so they overlap in the middle. Stick them together by scoring and applying slip on all the edges.

6 Next, bring the ends over the newspaper. You can fold the ends just to the top, or bring the ends to meet in the center. There's no right or wrong way. Score, apply slip, and smooth the edges.

7 Cut off any extra clay with your butter knife, or add a slab strip if you need more. Just remember to score and apply slip on all the connecting edges, especially if you are adding a new piece.

8 Next, seal all the sides with your thumb. When the project is fired in a kiln, you will end up with a hollow oval-shaped body.

9 Now repeat the process with a smaller slab of clay (about half the size) and more newspaper to create a round head about 2$\frac{1}{2}$ to 3 inches wide.

TURN THE PAGE

Q: My project is sagging or losing its shape. What should I do?

A: This can happen when your walls are not thick enough to support the weight of the sculpture as it grows. You can add more clay at the bottom to give it more support. In general, you should make your slabs thicker (about 3/4 inch) when forming the main body of your sculpture.

A: Losing the shape of your project can also occur when your clay is too wet, or if you have handled and or stretched it too much. In this case, it's best to make a new form with fresh clay.

A: If there is not enough crumpled newspaper inside your sculpture, your project may also sag. Make sure your newspaper is crumpled tightly together. If it's loose, it can't support your project.

Tip: If newspaper is showing through the clay, just patch the area with a small piece of clay by scoring, applying slip, and smoothing the area.

10 Next, you'll need to make some legs for your cat. Make four coils about 1 inch thick. Make them as tall as you like to match your cat.

11 Now put your cat together. Place the body so it is leaning at a slight angle, as shown in the picture. The front legs should be straight up and down to support the body at an angle. Be sure to score, apply slip, and seal the places where the legs and body attach.

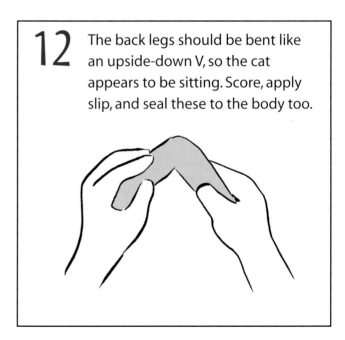

12 The back legs should be bent like an upside-down V, so the cat appears to be sitting. Score, apply slip, and seal these to the body too.

13  Next, make and attach the tail. It should be kept on the ground or very close to the body to prevent it from breaking.

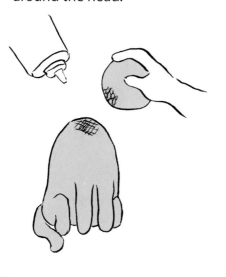

14 To attach the head to the body, you'll need to score and apply slip to the places where the head attaches to the body and the places where the body attaches to the head. Then firmly press the head and body together. Seal the edges around the head.

15 Now, roll out a new coil about $1/2$ inch thick. Place the coil between the head and the body and press it firmly to form a neck. Blend the clay smooth with your thumbs to complete your cat form.

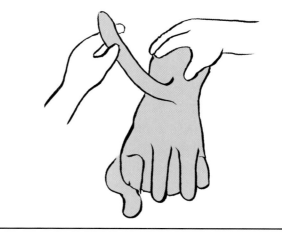

16 What will your cat's face look like? Get a small piece of clay and pinch out some clay ears. Then score and apply slip onto the head. Roll out some clay balls for a nose and two eyes.

TURN THE PAGE ➜

17 You can cut out a mouth with your butter knife. You can draw a mouth with your plastic-coated paper clip. You can make a small coil and build a mouth. It's your choice.

18 Next, have your adult helper cut the wire into 3-inch pieces for whiskers.

19 Then push three or four wires into side of the cat's face.

20 The final step is to poke a couple of holes in the hollow head and body with a plastic-coated paper clip. This will let the trapped steam escape in the kiln and will keep your project from cracking or exploding.

21 Use a pencil to write your name in your clay. Now you can decorate or dry your project.

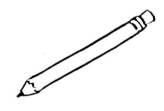

Floppy-Eared Dog by Chance

1 Follow steps 1 to 15 for the Sitting Cat on pages 48 to 51, but give your dog a short coil tail and make the head more oval than round.

2 To form the dog's snout, gently press down on the head just below where the eyes will go. Remember to support the underside of the head with your other hand.

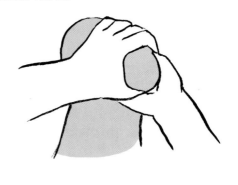

3 Cut a slit into the head to form the mouth. Then pull the top section up and the bottom section down. This will open your dog's mouth.

TURN THE PAGE

4 Make two floppy slab ears. Remember to score, apply slip, and press them firmly onto your dog's head.

5 To make teeth, roll small coils that look like carrots. Score the places where you want the teeth to go, apply slip, and press teeth into place.

6 Now you can draw in the eyes with a pencil or add clay eyes. Other details like a collar or bone in the mouth can be added too.

7 Remember to poke a hole in the hollow head and body with your plastic-coated paper clip.

8 Use a pencil to write your name in your clay. Now you can decorate or dry your project.

MYSTIC DRAGON

Mystic Dragon by Luke

1 Follow steps 1 to 12 for the Sitting Cat on pages 48 to 50.

2 Give your dragon a strong, mighty tail. Roll a big coil in the shape of an ice cream cone. You can bend it to the side or keep it straight. Don't forget to score, apply slip, and seal the tail and the body when you attach them.

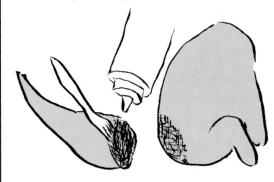

3 Before you attach the head to the body, you may want to make a long neck for your dragon. You can roll out a new slab to make a cylinder shape.

TURN THE PAGE →

4 Bunch and twist newspaper so that it's straight and as long as you want the neck to be.

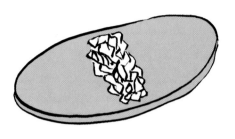

5 Roll your slab around and over the newspaper and trim off any extra clay. You can carefully bend this neck any way you want.

6 You'll need to score, apply slip, and smooth the places where the head attaches to the neck and where the neck attaches to the head. Also do this for the places where the neck and body attach. Then firmly press the head, neck, and body together.

7 Use a can or a jar to support the head and neck.

8 You can squeeze the clay to shape the nose and add some triangles down your dragon's back. Don't forget to score and apply slip!

9 To form the dragon's mouth, make a cut right below the nose. Add clay eyes, and you can add teeth if you like, too.

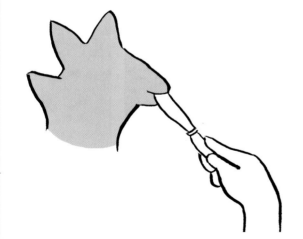

10 Use a paper clip to make air holes in the neck and body.

11 Use a pencil to write your name in your clay. Now you are ready to decorate or dry your project.

Hairy Bear by Alissa

1 Follow steps 1 to 10 for the Sitting Cat on pages 48 to 50. You should end up with these shapes:

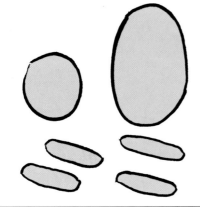

2 Now you can put your Hairy Bear together. To make your bear sit up straight, like a teddy bear, stand the body upright and attach straight coil legs and arms as shown here.

3 To attach the head to the body, you'll need to score and apply slip to the places where the head attaches to the body and where the body attaches to the head. Then firmly press the head and body together. Seal the edges around the head.

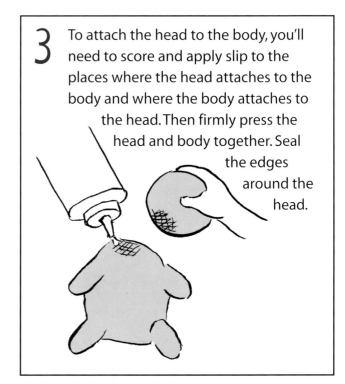

4 Now, roll out a new coil about $^1/_2$ inch thick. Place the coil between the head and the body. Press it firmly to form a neck. Blend the clay smooth with your thumbs to complete your bear form.

6 Draw lines on the body with a fork to create a hairy texture or add some soft clay and pinch out some fur.

5 Make some small round ears, a little nose, and two eyes. Then score, apply slip, and gently press them onto the head.

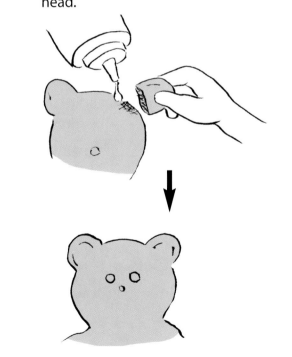

7 Use a pencil to write your name in your clay. Now you are ready to decorate or dry your project.

This method will show you how to make any project stand on legs or simply make your project tall. You will need to start with a project body.

Standing Fox by Sophia

1 Find a piece of foam that is large enough to support the body of your project. The foam should also lift your project as high as you'd want to build the legs.

2 Roll out thick coil legs. Then, score, apply slip, and seal them to the body. The foam supports the weight of the body while the legs dry.

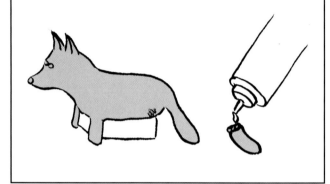

Tip: You should leave the foam in place until your project has been underglazed and transported to the kiln location for firing. Just before firing, someone will need to very carefully remove the foam. Squeezing the foam will make it smaller and easier to remove.

3 Use a pencil to write your name in your clay. Now you are ready to decorate or dry your project.

Prickly Porcupine by Vasudha

1 To make a porcupine, follow steps 1 to 9 for Sitting Cat on pages 48 to 49.

2 Lay the body flat on your board and attach the head by scoring and applying slip.

3 Create the legs and then see Standing Animal on page 60 to see how to make your porcupine stand up.

4 Next, add eyes and a mouth. (You could add a pointy nose too.) Don't forget to score and apply slip!

TURN THE PAGE

5 Last, add your wire. Have your adult helper cut 25 to 30 pieces of wire, each about 2¹/₂ to 3 inches long.

6 Push the wire into the body every where but the head.

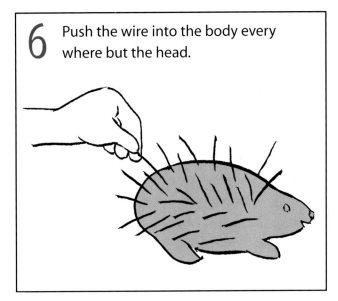

7 Use a pencil to write your name in your clay. Now you are ready to decorate or dry your project.

ABSTRACT SHAPES

What would your favorite color look like if it was a shape? What if you combined a dog and a butterfly, or a mountain and a person? Or maybe there is a shape that you like and it has no special meaning at all. These could all be ideas for abstract sculptures. Abstract art doesn't look like your thoughts in any real way. It's a way of showing your feelings or ideas freely with shapes and forms. Each person who looks at an abstract sculpture may see something different.

Possible Projects

Interesting Forms

Flat and Bumpy Landscapes

You Will Need:

- canvas-covered board to work on

- white low-fire clay

- cut-off tool to cut your clay

- scrap foam (available from local foam stores) to use as support

- newspaper to crumple and support clay

- rolling pin to roll out clay slabs

- ruler to measure thickness of clay

- fork to score clay

- slip to attach pieces together

- medium paint brush (or plastic squeeze bottle) to apply slip

- bowl of water to wet hands

- butter knife or fettling knife to cut clay

- sponge to smooth your project

- plastic-coated paper clip to check thickness of clay

- plastic wrap or dry-cleaning bags to prevent your project from drying (optional)

Sculpture by Matthew

1 Find different-shaped pieces of foam to use as molds: cylinders, squares, rectangles, or cones.

2 Roll out a slab about 3/4 inch thick and large enough to wrap around the foam you like.

3 Now mold the slab around the foam. Pull the sides of the slab up and over the foam and attach them together by scoring and applying slip to the edges.

4 You could also close up one end over the foam—it's your choice!

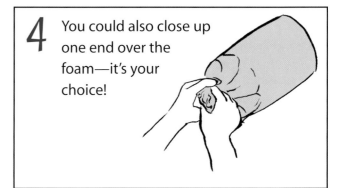

5 Remember to leave one side open so you can pull the foam out later.

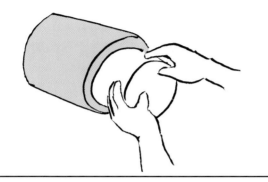

6 You should end up with a hollow shape that looks like the foam.

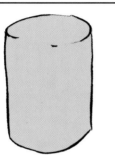

7 You can attach this shape to a slab base, make it stand higher with legs, or simply use it to begin building your sculpture. (See page 60 for information on making a standing project.)

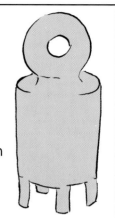

8 Use a pencil to write your name in your clay. Now you can decorate or dry your project.

Landscape Sculpture by Emma

1 To make a flat base, roll out a flat slab.

2 You can also make a bumpy rolling landscape by placing your flat slab over pieces of foam or bunched newspaper. (Keep the foam underneath until it is ready to fire.)

3 Look around you. You can make anything you see out of clay. Then add it to your base.

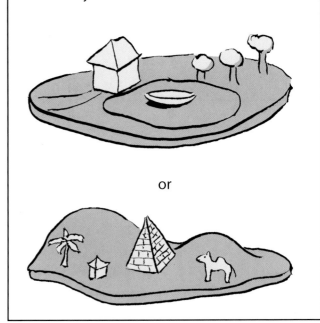

or

4 Use a pencil to write your name in your clay. Now you can decorate or dry your project.

4

Wheel-Throwing Projects

Chelsea uses both hands to slowly pull up the walls of her pot on the electric potter's wheel.

WHEEL-THROWING PROJECTS

I pretend to be a mayor seeing a large skyscraper rise.
Now the part I've been waiting for has finally come: I can shape my pot.—Galen

I feel I need to throw a pot right now!—Alicia

Learning to Use the Potter's Wheel

Working on the potter's wheel is one of the most exciting skills to learn. The speed of the spinning wheel allows you to center a ball of clay, so you can form thin-walled projects that are even in thickness on all sides. Once the side walls are pulled up into a cylinder shape, you can transform it into one of many objects, like a tall vase or a wide bowl.

This chapter begins with some basic wheel-throwing lessons and tips. Then you'll learn how to make cylindrical, curved, and flat projects on the potter's wheel with wet clay. There are six projects in all. You'll also learn about trimming your leather-hard project on the potter's wheel. Then, go to chapter 5 to learn about decorating tips, underglazing and glazing methods, and firing options to complete your project.

Wheel-Throwing Tips for Helpers

Many people believe that wheel-throwing is too difficult for children to learn, but the results at Kids 'N' Clay Pottery Studio have proven otherwise. The difference is guiding children through a simpler process that they can understand and successfully accomplish. As you will soon see, your hands-on involvement and guidance is an important part of the learning process.

This chapter includes five lessons highlighting skills that build on one another. The first three lessons focus on basic throwing, while the last two focus on finishing up a project on the wheel. It is important to have a wet, wheel-thrown project still attached to the wheel before moving on to lesson four.

Before you begin, make sure that your child is comfortable and familiar with the key parts of the potter's wheel so they can concentrate on learning how to throw. For this reason, an electric potter's wheel is recommended for beginners. For more information on finding a potter's wheel, see "Studio Materials & Supplies" on page 3 or "Finding a Local Supplier" on page xi.

Time Tips for Helpers

Please be aware that these wheel-throwing projects cannot be completed in a single day. Most projects are created in the four stages as listed on page 6. You should allow enough time to get through the following steps:

- On the first day, throw the main body

- On the second day, trim and decorate

- Underglaze when the project is leather-hard or bone-dry; see chapter 5

- Bisque-fire the project once it is bone-dry

- After bisque-firing, the project can be glazed and glaze-fired

GETTING TO KNOW YOUR WHEEL

Before you get started, you need to get familiar with your potter's wheel and review some important safety rules. There are two types of wheels that you can use—an electric wheel or a foot-powered kick-wheel. It's best to start with an electric wheel that you don't have to spin yourself. Make sure

7. Stool

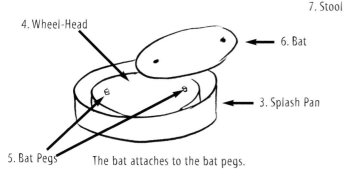

4. Wheel-Head
6. Bat
3. Splash Pan
5. Bat Pegs

The bat attaches to the bat pegs.

that you can find each of these key areas on the electric wheel that you will be using.

1. The *On/Off Switch* turns the power on and off.

2. The *Foot Pedal* controls the speed of the wheel.

3. The *Splash Pan* captures extra water and clay.

4. The *Wheel-Head* is the work surface that spins.

5. If your wheel-head has *Bat Pegs,* you will attach your bat to them.

6. The *Bat* is the removable work surface.

7. An easy-to-clean *Stool* or *Chair* will bring you close to the wheel.

8. Is the *Power Cord* plugged into the electrical outlet? Ask for help if it's not.

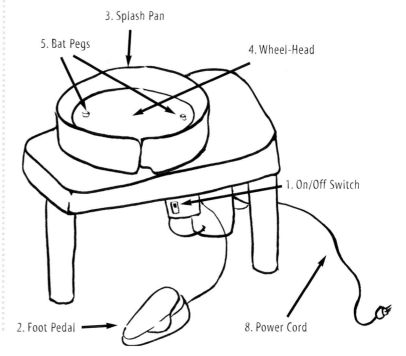

3. Splash Pan
5. Bat Pegs
4. Wheel-Head
1. On/Off Switch
2. Foot Pedal
8. Power Cord

1. Know how to use your wheel before you begin. (Ask for help if you need it.)

2. Always shut off your wheel when you are not using it (even if it's just for a minute).

3. Expect to get messy. Wear clothes that can be easily washed or wear a smock.

4. Keep loose, hanging things away from the wheel, so they won't get caught. Roll up your sleeves, tie back long hair, and keep your work area uncluttered.

5. Always use a bat if your wheel-head has pegs (even for trimming).

6. Never put your hands in the splash pan when the wheel is spinning.

7. Always keep your hands wet and slippery when you are throwing on the wheel.

8. Pay attention to what you are doing when you are working on the wheel.

9. Move your hands in slow motion, especially when moving them off and on the clay.

10. Always shut off your wheel before you begin to clean it.

Five Basic Lessons

This chapter teaches five basic skills you will need for every wheel-throwing project. These skills are:
1. Preparing your clay
2. Attaching your clay to the wheel-head or bat
3. Centering your clay
   (This is the point at which you will learn to throw various shapes.)
4. Cutting your project off the wheel
5. Trimming the bottom of your project

You will need to complete Lessons 1, 2, and 3 before you can create your project. You can only do Lesson 4 while your project is still stuck to the wheel-head or bat. Do Lesson 5 after your project becomes leather-hard.

You Will Need:

■ canvas-covered board to work on

■ white low-fire clay

■ cut-off tool to cut clay

■ electric potter's wheel

■ bat (for pegged wheel-heads)

■ bowl of water to wet your hands

■ plastic-coated paper clip to poke holes in clay

■ sponge to soak up extra water

LESSON 1: PREPARING YOUR CLAY

To prevent your clay from separating or cracking on the potter's wheel or in the kiln, you need to remove all the air bubbles. Make sure that all your clay is mixed well together before attaching it to the potter's wheel. This process is called "wedging." Be sure that your work surface is clean before you start.

1 Cut off a piece of clay that is large enough to fill the palm of your hand when you form a ball.

2 Throw your ball of clay down on the canvas-covered board about 20 times. Turn it slightly each time you throw it down so a different side hits the table.

3 Then pat the clay back into a ball again.

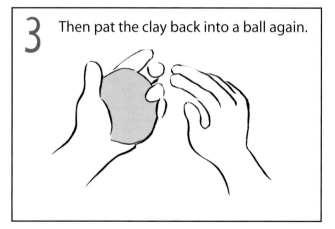

4 Now you're ready to attach your clay to the potter's wheel.

How you attach your clay to the wheel-head is very important. You don't want the clay to become loose while you are working on the wheel. A little water and a little muscle are the key ingredients for securely attaching clay.

1 Make sure your wheel is off.

2 If the wheel-head has bat pegs, attach a bat.

3 Moisten a wood bat or the metal wheel-head with water using your fingertips. This will make the clay stick better.

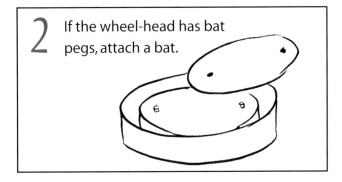

4 Slam your ball of clay into the middle of your wheel-head as hard as you can.

5 Then push and pat the clay into a rounded beehive shape in the center of the wheel-head.

LESSON 3: CENTERING YOUR CLAY

Getting all your clay centered in the middle of the wheel-head is the secret to beginning every wheel-throwing project. When centered, your clay should spin without any bumps or wobbles. Centering can be difficult when you are first learning. It takes lots of practice to master this skill. Even the most experienced potters have days when centering is hard, so don't worry if you can't get it exactly. When you get close, just move on to the next step. Once you've learned how to center your clay, you can begin your first cylinder project.

Centering Tips for Helpers

It is imperative that you assist your child when they are learning how to center. Wheel-throwing knowledge is not required for assisting. However, those with pottery experience will need to pay attention to the differences in these techniques from standard adult practices. These instructions have been purposely simplified to eliminate the need for additional tools. Your child's hands are used as the primary tools whenever possible. Also, please note the role of the sponge in children's ceramics. It is only used to absorb water and not for wetting the clay. Only hands are used to wet the clay. This prevents the use of too much water when throwing, which can become extremely messy and uncontrollable for children.

1 Once your wedged clay is attached to your wheel, sit as close as you can to the wheel.

2 Turn the wheel on.

3 Press the foot pedal down and notice the change in speed from slow to fast. Adjust the pedal until you find a medium speed for centering. Then take your foot off the pedal to keep this speed constant.

4 Wet the clay with your hands and wet your hands again.

TURN THE PAGE →

5 Make sure that your hands stay slippery and wet. As soon as they start getting sticky, slowly take them off the clay and wet them again.

6 Cup both hands around the clay with your thumbs close together or even touching.

7 Lock your arms against the edge of the splash pan.

8 Now lean in, bending from the waist, and slowly push the clay in toward the center with both hands.

Lev demonstrates the correct body position for centering.

9 Begin shifting the clay more toward the center by pushing down and forward.

Q: I'm not strong enough to center the clay. My hands just keep moving around.

A: Body position is more important than strength. Make sure that you are sitting as close as possible to the wheel. Both arms need to be locked against the splash pan to get the right angle. When leaning forward, bend from the waist and push with your whole body not just your hands.

Centering Tips for Helpers

As your child is centering the clay, sit across from them. Have them push the clay toward you, as you use one hand to push the clay toward them. This combination of pressure will usually center the clay quickly. Make sure that you keep your hand wet when you are assisting.

Alissa helps Lev center his clay.

10 After pushing in a little, a small bump or layer of clay may form at the bottom of the clay ball.

Use the fingernail on your thumb to scrape away the extra clay. Keep your fingernail against the wheel or bat where the extra clay first formed and push in until all the extra clay is removed.

11 Now wet your hands again and continue to push the clay inward until it no longer wobbles.

TURN THE PAGE ↗

12 Keep repeating steps 8 to 11 until you've formed a dome shape with no wobbles.

Q: My piece of clay came off the wheel-head. What should I do?

A: With the wheel turned off, throw your clay back down onto the wheel-head. It should stick, but you'll have to center it again. Make sure your hands are slippery and wet, and press down toward the wheel-head as you center. If your hands are not wet enough, they can stick to the clay and pull it off the wheel-head again.

13 To test if your clay is centered, loosely drape your wet fingers around the top of your clay. If your fingers wobble, you're still off center. If they stay in place, you've centered your clay!

Q: I keep trying and trying and I can't get my clay centered. What should I do?

A: If you are having problems mastering centering, don't worry. If your clay is almost centered, just move on to the next step. The project may end up slightly thicker on one side, but creativity is the goal, not perfection. With more practice, centering will become easier.

Cylinder Projects

You'll begin your first wheel-throwing project by creating a simple cylinder form (or tube shape) with straight walls. Remember to move in slow motion as you are working. Pulling up the side walls is the main skill you will be learning here. You will notice the outward pull felt by spinning objects. This is known as centrifugal force and it pushes the walls out. You'll learn how to keep your walls straight in the two possible projects that are described here.

Cylinder Project Tip for Helpers

There will be many learning mistakes when your child first starts using the wheel. It's important to set up the proper expectation, so that your child is not too disappointed if a project collapses, moves off center, or comes off the wheel. The important thing is to learn from those errors and just start over. Similar to riding a bike, taking a few falls is a natural part of the learning process.

Once your child finishes throwing a cylinder project, the project will need to be removed from the wheel-head. This skill is covered in "Lesson 4: Cutting Your Project Off the Wheel" on page 82. When the project is leather-hard, your child can move on to "Lesson 5: Trimming the Bottom" on pages 83 to 86.

You Will Need:

- canvas-covered board to work on
- white low-fire clay
- cut-off tool to cut clay
- electric potter's wheel
- bat (for pegged wheel-heads)
- bowl of water to wet your hands
- plastic-coated paper clip to poke holes in clay
- sponge to soak up extra water
- ruler to measure thickness of clay
- spatula or paint scraper to lift your project off the wheel (optional)
- plastic wrap or dry-cleaning bag to prevent your project from drying
- slip to attach pieces
- medium paint brush (or plastic squeeze bottle) to apply slip
- small board to dry your project
- pencil to draw trimming guidelines on bat or wheel-head

Possible Projects

Pencil Holders

Cocoa Mugs

Everyone needs a place to put pens and pencils. A pencil holder is a basic cylinder form that can even be used as a cup or a toothbrush holder.

Pencil Holder by Natalie

1 Center a medium piece of clay that fits well in the palm of your hand by following the steps on pages 73 to 76.

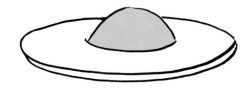

2 Wet your hands and press your thumbs together to form a butterfly shape. Your thumbs should be side by side touching each other.

3 Now gently put your hands around the clay dome.

4

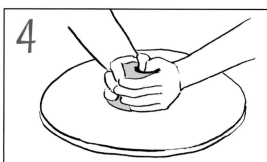

Slowly press your thumbs down into the center of the clay to form a small well. Make sure that your thumbs stay stiff and pressed together, or you won't be pressing down in the center. Stop when you are about $1/2$ inch from the bottom.

Q: It's hard to push my thumbs down the center. I feel stickiness and pulling.

A: Make sure that your thumbs are locked together, body position is correct, and that your hands are slippery and wet at all times. That may mean rewetting your hands just moments after touching the clay.

Assisting Tip for Helpers:

If a small bump forms in the middle of the well when your child is pushing their thumbs down into the clay, have them gently press the bump down with one thumb and continue making the well. This happens when fingernails are too long or when thumbs are not close enough together.

5 To check the thickness of the bottom, straighten the end of your plastic-coated paper clip and use it to push through the bottom of your clay. Note where it hits the bottom, and meaure it with a ruler.

6 To make the bottom of your pencil holder and start the wall, put one hand on top of the other inside the well. Then gently pull the clay toward you with your fingertips. Stop pulling when the wall is about $3/4$ inch thick.

TURN THE PAGE

7 Wet your hands again and gently push the top part of your clay in toward the center to keep your wall straight. This is called *collaring*.

8 Now you are going to form the side walls by pulling up the clay. Make the butterfly shape again, but this time cross your thumbs.

9 Then put one hand inside the well and one hand outside.

Your inside hand should start at the bottom, and your outside hand should start near the bat or wheel-head.

10 Very slowly and gently squeeze the clay evenly between your inside fingertips and your outside fingertips while pulling up.

11 Repeat step 10 several times until the wall is between $1/2$ inch and $1/4$ inch thick. It is important to collar the wall after each pull, as shown in Step 7.

12 After your wall is complete, use your fingers as shown to create a straight edge on top.

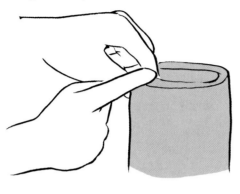

14 To cut your project off the wheel-head, go to page 82 and follow all the steps.

15 Once your project is leather-hard, trim the bottom as shown on pages 83 to 86.

13 Carefully use your sponge to soak up any extra water inside, and turn off your wheel.

16 Use a pencil to write your name in your clay. Now you can decorate or dry your project.

Removal Tip for Helpers

We strongly recommend that you assist your child with cutting the project off the wheel. See Lesson 4 on the next page. The key is keeping the string tight against the bat as it drags through the bottom of the project.

LESSON 4: CUTTING YOUR PROJECT OFF THE WHEEL

After throwing every project, you will need to cut it off the wheel-head or bat so it won't be stuck when it dries. This last step must be done very carefully. You don't want to cut into the project itself by mistake. Ask for adult help, especially the first time you try this.

You Will Need:

- electric potter's wheel
- wet wheel-thrown project stuck to bat or wheel-head
- cut-off tool to remove project from bat or wheel-head
- spatula or paint scraper for lifting project
- small board for storing project

1 The wheel should be spinning at the slowest speed for small projects. Turn it off if your project is large.

2

Shorten the string on your cut-off tool by wrapping it around the wooden handles. The string should be 2 inches longer than the base of your project on both sides.

3 Put the cut-off tool flat against the bat or wheel-head behind your project and pull the handles outward. Keep the string very tight and press down on the string with your thumbs.

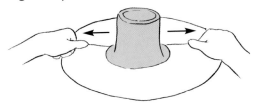

4 Now slowly but firmly pull the tool toward you. This will separate your project from the bat or wheel-head so you can lift it up when it dries.

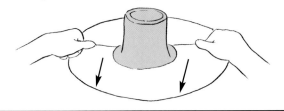

5 If you are using a bat, lift the bat off the wheel and let your project dry until it is leather-hard. If you are cutting your project off the wheel-head, use a spatula or a paint scraper to lift your project onto a small board where it can dry. When your project is leather-hard, you'll trim it as shown on the next page.

LESSON 5: TRIMMING THE BOTTOM

Trimming removes the extra weight at the bottom of wheel-thrown projects and forms a curve and a small foot on the bottom. It's called a "foot" because that's what your pot stands on. You create a foot by trimming the bottom of your pot on the wheel-head when it is at the leather-hard stage. You'll be using different-shaped trimming tools and a few pieces of wet clay to hold your project in place. When you first start trimming, draw a trimming guide on your bat or wheel-head to help you center your project. After a few times, you won't have to do this.

Daron trims a pot.

You Will Need:

- leather-hard project
- electric potter's wheel
- scrap clay to hold your project in place
- bowl of water to wet your hands
- three trimming tools to trim bottom of project
- ruler to measure thickness of clay
- pencil to write your name on bottom of project

1 Figure out how thick the bottom of your pot is by putting one finger on the inside bottom and one on the outside bottom at the same time. This will tell you how much you can trim off without cutting through the bottom of your pot. Each time you do this, it will get easier to tell how thick the bottom is.

TURN THE PAGE

2   To draw a trimming guide, use a pencil to draw a series of circles on the bat or on the wheel-head while it is spinning

3   Turn the wheel off and place your pot or plate upside down on the bat or wheel-head using the pencil guides to help you center.

4   Turn the wheel on slow speed.

5   If your pot is not centered, gently tap your pot so it moves. The spinning of the wheel should help pull the pot to the center.

6   A centered pot moves in a perfect circle in the middle of the wheel-head. You'll need to find the right pressure of tapping. Adult help is important here.

7   Once your project is centered, shut off the wheel and carefully moisten the area right around the rim of the pot.

8 Make coils with scraps of clay.

9 Hold the bottom of the pot so it doesn't move and put the coils around the pot (but don't press too hard or your rim can break). The idea is to have the coils hold your pot in place while you trim.

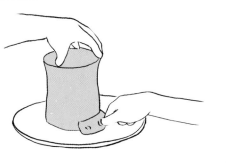

10 Turn your wheel on medium speed.

Tip: If your rim is decorated, you'll have to be extra careful when you put the coils on the pot.

11 Hold your trimming tool with both hands, press your arms against the splash pan, and press the tool against the top edge of the bottom of your pot. The way you move your tool will shape your pot's bottom.

Galen trims a foot on his pot.

12 To carve out a foot, use the corner of your trimming tool to mark where you would like the outside of your foot to begin. Hold the trimming tool firm and still in one spot and let the movement of the wheel help shave away the clay.

TURN THE PAGE

Tip: You want to trim the extra clay away without going through the bottom of your pot. If you think you are getting close to the inside bottom, take your coils off and check to see where you are (see step 1). If you need to trim more, you'll have to repeat steps 3 to 10 before you trim again.

13 After the outside edge is complete, you will need to shave inside the foot area too. This will be a big area if you are trimming a plate. You should start trimming from the very center and work your way out to the inside edge of the foot. A spiral design sometimes forms on the bottom when you trim.

Sarah trims a foot.

14 When you are finished, shut off the wheel, carefully remove the coils, and remove your pot.

15 Next you can attach handles, a spout, or other details to your project.

16 Use a pencil to write your name in your clay. Now you are ready to decorate or dry your project.

COCOA MUG

Hot cocoa with marshmallows is a wonderful afternoon treat when it's served in a ceramic mug you made yourself. This project is similar to Pencil Holder, but you'll add fancy handles that make a big difference in both how it looks and how it feels in your hand. Try making a few different styles of handles before you attach them. You can adjust the width of the mug by using a bigger or smaller piece of clay to form the base.

Cocoa Mug by Rachel

1 Follow steps 1 to 13 for a Pencil Holder on pages 78 to 81. See page 82 for how to cut your cylinder off the wheel.

2 Let your cylinder dry overnight until it becomes leather-hard.

3 Trim the bottom as shown on pages 83 to 86.

4 Make a fancy coil handle about 1/2 inch thick. You can flatten it slightly by pressing it down on the table. You can also gently run your wet finger along the top side of the coil to flatten it a little bit.

5 Bend it into the shape you want. Then score and apply slip to the ends of the handle and to the places on the mug where the handle will attach. Press and smooth the handle in place.

6 Use a pencil to write your name in your clay. Now you are ready to decorate or dry your project.

Curved Projects

Making curves on the potter's wheel can be a lot of fun because the shape of your project changes so quickly. Once you know how to make curves on the wheel, you can create lots of interesting forms and different kinds of containers. To make curves, you first throw a simple cylinder form, like the Pencil Holder. Then, you carefully push the clay in or out to create beautiful curves for bowls, vases, pitchers, and more.

You Will Need:

- canvas-covered board to work on
- white low-fire clay
- cut-off tool to cut clay
- electric potter's wheel
- bat (for pegged wheel-heads)
- bowl of water to wet your hands
- plastic-coated paper clip to poke holes in clay
- sponge to soak up extra water
- ruler to measure thickness of clay
- spatula or paint scraper to lift your project off the wheel (optional)
- plastic wrap or dry-cleaning bags to prevent your project from drying

- slip to attach pieces
- medium paint brush (or plastic squeeze bottle) to apply slip
- small board to dry your project
- pencil to draw trimming guidelines on bat or wheel

Curved Project Tips for Helpers

Remind your child of the importance of moving in slow motion when working with a potter's wheel, especially when lifting fingertips off the clay. It's easy to accidentally bump into the project when you're moving quickly, which can push the project off center. Collaring and pushing the clay toward the center may bring the project back to center if it hasn't shifted too far; otherwise, your child will have to recenter a new piece of clay.

Possible Projects

Fruit Bowl

Curved Vase

Orange Juice Pitcher

FRUIT BOWL

When you form this large Fruit Bowl, you'll learn how to make wide outward curves on the potter's wheel. Creating a wide base on your cylinder will allow the bowl to hold more. It's great for displaying whole fruit like apples, oranges, and bananas, or for serving a fruit salad.

Fruit Bowl by Megan

1 Center a large piece of clay about the size of a grapefruit.

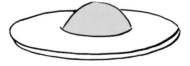

2 Follow steps 2 to 12 for the Pencil Holder on pages 78 to 81 to form a cylinder shape with a wide base about 5 or 6 inches across.

Tip: The walls will get thinner when you add the curves, so be careful not to make the walls too thin or they will not be able to stand up (1/4 inch is as thin as you should go—1/2 inch in thickness is best). If your walls begin to sag or fall, simply start over with some fresh clay.

3 To make a bowl, you need to form an outward curve. Position your hands as if you were going to pull up the walls again, but this time press gently outward with your inside hand. Your outside hand should just support the clay. It may take a few pulls to get the shape you want.

TURN THE PAGE →

Tip: If you bring the walls too far over the base, they may collapse.

4 Once you have shaped the bowl the way you want, smooth the top edge using your index finger as shown.

5 Carefully use your sponge to soak up any extra water inside, and turn off your wheel.

6 To cut your project off the wheel, go to page 82 and follow all the steps.

7 Trim your pot as shown on pages 83 to 86.

8 Use a pencil to write your name in your clay. Now you are ready to decorate or dry your project.

CURVED VASE

This Curved Vase project will combine the outward curve that you learned in the Fruit Bowl project with an inward curve that will form the narrow neck of the vase. You can make one of each curve for a simple vase, or make many alternating inward and outward curves to create a fancy wave design.

Curved Vase by Rachel

2 Follow steps 2 to 11 for Pencil Holder on page 78 to 81 to form a cylinder shape with a narrow base about 3 or 4 inches across.

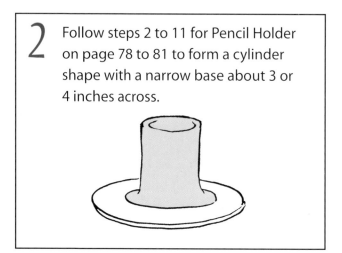

Tip: Pull up your walls a little bit taller than you want your vase to be, because making curves will make the walls shorter. Also, remember that the walls will get thinner when you add curves. Be careful not to make the walls too thin or they will not be able to stand up (1/4 inch is as thin as you should go—1/2 inch in thickness is best). If your walls begin to sag or fall, simply start over with some fresh clay.

1 Center a large piece of clay about the size of a grapefruit.

TURN THE PAGE

3 To make a vase, you can form an outward curve on the bottom. Position your hands as if you were going to pull up the walls again, but this time press gently outward with your inside hand. Your outside hand should just support the clay. It may take a few pulls to get the shape you want.

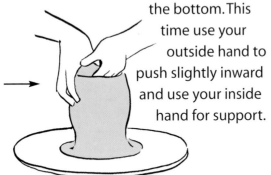

4 To make a narrow neck for a vase, make an inward curve. Wet your hands again and start with a new pull from the bottom. This time use your outside hand to push slightly inward and use your inside hand for support.

You can also collar the clay around the neck area.

5 Once you have shaped the vase or the bowl the way you want, smooth the top edge using your index finger as shown.

6 Carefully use your sponge to soak up any extra water inside, and turn off your wheel.

7 To cut your project off the wheel, follow all the steps on page 82.

8 Trim your pot as shown on pages 83 to 86.

9 Use a pencil to write your name in your clay. Now you are ready to decorate or dry your project.

ORANGE JUICE PITCHER

This Orange Juice Pitcher is basically a Curved Vase with a spout and a handle and is great for serving juice, tea, punch, or ice water. You can make a small spout or dramatic large one. You'll start with the basic Pencil Holder or cylinder shape, then make both an outward and an inward curve to make the vase shape.

Orange Juice Pitcher by Hillary

1 Follow steps 1 to 6 for the Curved Vase on pages 91 to 92.

2 To make a spout, make sure that your wheel is off. Use your fingers to form a small spout while the clay is still soft, or see step 4.

3 Cut your project off the wheel-head or bat as shown on page 82. When it is leather-hard, trim the bottom as shown on pages 83 to 86.

TURN THE PAGE ➔

4 (Optional) For a large spout, use the pinch or coil method to create a separate spout. This spout will be attached by scoring and applying slip when your pot has reached the leather-hard stage and has already been trimmed.

5 Make a coil handle any shape you like. (See step 4 on page 87 for an idea.)

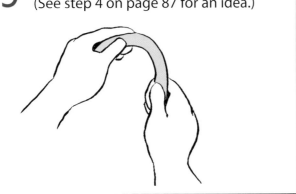

6 Score and apply slip to the surface of the pitcher and the ends of the handle. Then press and smooth the handle in place.

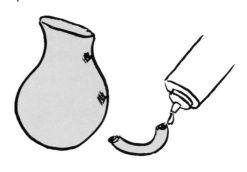

7 Use a pencil to write your name in your clay. Now you are ready to decorate or dry your project.

Flat Projects

Flat projects are like short cylinder projects, but you'll be working much closer to the wheel and using a lot more clay. Instead of making a beehive shape for centering, you'll make your clay look more like a little hill or a dome. Also, when you are throwing a plate, the bottom is thrown very thick, which means a lot of clay will be trimmed away later.

You Will Need:

- canvas-covered board to work on
- white low-fire clay
- cut-off tool to cut clay
- electric potter's wheel
- bat (for pegged wheel-heads)
- bowl of water to wet your hands
- plastic-coated paper clip to poke holes in clay
- sponge to soak up extra water
- ruler to measure thickness of clay
- spatula or paint scraper to lift your project off the wheel (optional)

- plastic wrap or dry-cleaning bags to prevent your project from drying
- slip to attach pieces
- medium paint brush (or plastic squeeze bottle) to apply slip
- small board to dry your project
- pencil to draw trimming guidelines on bat or wheel

Flat Project Tips for Helpers

When centering flat projects, you'll want to direct your child to push down rather than pushing forward. The clay will be centered much lower and wider. The base will also be much thicker and more difficult to cut off the wheel, so adult assistance will be important.

Possible Projects

Snack Dishes

Dessert Plates

SNACK DISHES & DESSERT PLATES

This plate is perfect for bite-size snacks or your favorite dessert. You can keep it simple or decorate it with festive holiday and seasonal designs. If you made a Cocoa Mug earlier, you could make a matching saucer now.

Dessert Plate by Morgan

Snack Dish by Tonio

1 First center your clay as you would for a cylinder.

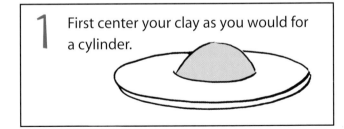

2 To flatten the clay, cup one hand around the side of the dome shape. Hold your other hand out like in a karate chop and press your palm against your first hand. Press your little finger against the top of the dome and push down against the clay.

3 When the clay is 1¹/₂ inches thick, open a well by slowly pressing your thumbs down into the center of the clay.

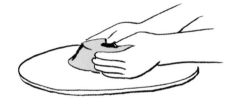

4 Stop the wheel and poke the bottom of your clay well with a paper clip to check the thickness. It should be about 1 inch thick.

5 Put one hand on top of the other inside the well and gently pull the clay toward you with your fingertips. Stop when the outside wall is 1/2 inch thick.

6 Pull the wall up just a little to create the plate rim.

7 Then angle the rim outward using both hands as shown.

8 Smooth the edge with your wet fingers.

9 Once you have shaped the plate the way you want, you'll need to cut your project off the wheel-head. Follow all the steps on page 82.

10 Let your project dry to leather-hard. Then trim the bottom as shown on pages 83 to 86.

11 Use a pencil to write your name in your clay. Now you are ready to decorate or dry your project.

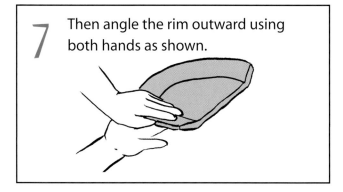

5

Decorating, Surface Treatments, & Firings

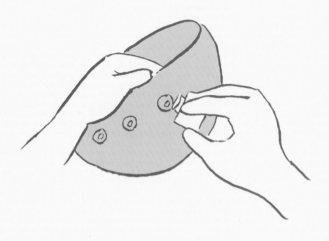

Gabe paints the walls of his castle fountain with colored underglaze before it is fired in the kiln.

99

DECORATING, SURFACE TREATMENTS, & FIRINGS

I love to put the paint on thick so it drips down the sides. —Eliza

It's fun. It makes your stuff really shiny and beautiful. —Lily

The Final Touches

Adding extra designs and color to the surface of your project are the creative details that really bring your project to life. This chapter describes five ways you can decorate with clay:

- Create designs on the surface of the clay

- Draw or paint designs with underglazes

- Dip or paint your project with low-fire glazes

- Burnish your project for a shiny look

- Smoke-fire your project for an ancient look

Please read about each of these methods before you begin drying or decorating your project. You can use many of these decorating methods together or just use low-fire glazing. It's interesting to experiment with different glazes and firings. Each time you try something it comes out of the kiln a little different. That's the mysterious thing about working with glazes and firings. The final result is always a surprise!

Decorating Tips for Helpers

Most kids think of decorating ideas when they are building their projects. All they need is access to glazes, a few tools, and some general guidance on what techniques they can use at each stage. It's important they decide which decorating methods they want to use before they begin drying their project. As you will see, different effects and approaches are used at various stages of drying. There are wide variety of colorful, nontoxic underglazes and glazes available. See "A Note for Parents and Teachers" on page xi to learn about ceramic suppliers and places to fire your child's finished work in a kiln.

Decorating in Clay

When you press into the clay, make sure that you always support the back side of the clay wall with your hand or, for flat projects, with a hard surface.

Will presses a shell into soft clay.

You Will Need:

- newspaper to cover glaze area
- canvas-covered board to work on
- a project with soft or leather-hard clay
- extra clay for making designs
- bowl of water for wetting hands
- pencil or plastic-coated paper clip for drawing designs
- slip in a squeeze bottle
- rubber stamps for making designs in clay
- cookie cutters for cutting out objects (optional)
- wooden tool to decorate the edges
- trimming tool for carving
- fettling knife to cut clay

DECORATING IN SOFT CLAY

1 When your clay is wet, you can press rubber stamps or other objects into the soft clay.

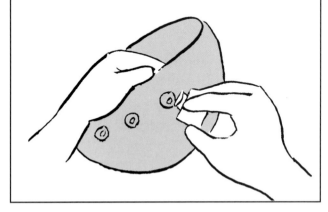

2 You can even use a pencil to draw lines or other designs into the clay.

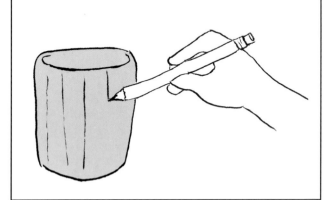

3 You can also make small objects by hand or cut some out with a cookie cutter. Score and apply slip to them, then gently press them onto the surface of your project. For example, if you are making a Fruit Bowl, you could attach small pieces of clay fruit to the surface of your bowl.

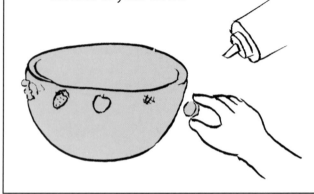

Elena draws lines in soft clay.

DECORATING IN LEATHER-HARD CLAY

1 Once your clay is leather-hard, you can carve more detailed designs into the stiff clay.

2 Another interesting technique is drawing designs with slip. You can make designs by squeezing the slip out of a bottle or by dabbing it on with a plastic-coated paper clip. The end result is a raised design on the surface of the clay.

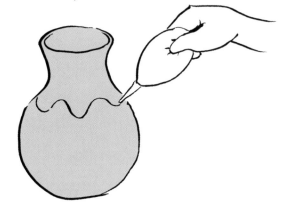

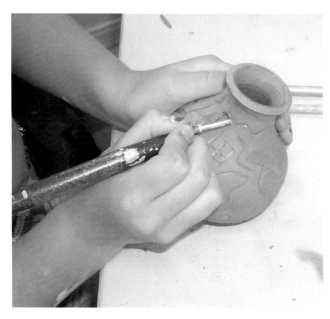

Sophia carves into a leather-hard pot.

Drawing & Painting with Underglaze

Underglaze is a mixture of clay, stains, and oxides. It's called "underglaze" because this layer is normally under the glaze coating. This is how you make designs on your clay before it is fired for the first time.

Liquid underglazes can be applied on wet clay, leather-hard clay, or bone-dry clay. You can use paintbrushes, sponges, or a toothbrush and your thumb to splatter the underglaze. When you put the underglaze on in different stages of drying, you'll get different looks in the end.

When your underglazed project is bone-dry, it will be fired. (This first firing is called the bisque.) Bisque-fired projects will not be water proof and they should not be used for food yet. See page 107 to learn about low-fire glazing if you'd like to use your project to hold food.

Underglazing Tips for Helpers

It is especially important that you understand the difference between the underglaze process and the low-fire glaze process. Underglazes are applied to unfired work or greenware and are bisque-fired to cone 04. Low-fire glazes are applied to projects that have already been bisque-fired. They are then fired to cone 06, so the glaze melts and covers the clay with a waterproof surface.

When you purchase underglazes and glazes, please read the label carefully to make sure they are nontoxic (contain no lead). Glazes are available in premixed jars that are ready for painting.

You Will Need:

- newspaper to put under your project
- an unfired project at any stage of drying
- nontoxic underglazes
- variety of paintbrushes to apply the underglaze
- bowl of water to rinse your paint brushes
- sponges to wipe the bottom of your project
- toothbrush for spattering (optional)
- underglaze pencils to draw on designs (optional)
- a place to bisque-fire your work

UNDERGLAZING ON WET CLAY

Apply underglaze with a paintbrush to make brush strokes or blurry designs in the underglaze.

1 Open and stir the underglaze mixture.

2 Apply 2 or 3 coats to make your design, but do not paint the bottom.

Ezra demonstrates painting underglaze on wet clay.

UNDERGLAZING ON LEATHER-HARD CLAY

You can try a special method called sgraffito. Once you apply your underglaze, you scrape away a design in the underglaze with a pencil or paper clip to uncover the clay body underneath. (Don't worry, any pencil marks you make will burn away in the firing.)

1 Open and stir the underglaze mixture.

2 Apply 2 or 3 coats to your project, except for the bottom.

3 After the underglaze dries, use a pencil or plastic-coated paper clip to scrape a design in the glaze.

Ezra demonstrates sgraffito.

If you would like to cover your entire project with underglazes, you should wait until your project is bone-dry. Painting underglaze is great for large projects or more detailed designs. You can use as many different colors as you like to make your design, and you can even put one color on top of another.

1   Open and stir the underglaze mixture.

2   Apply 2 or 3 coats to cover your whole project, except for the bottom.

Will demonstrates painting underglaze on bone-dry clay.

Low-Fire Glazing

Low-fire glaze is a type of liquid glass that melts and coats the clay when it is fired. After your project has been glaze-fired, it is safe for food and drinks. However, you should hand-wash your projects. The dishwasher—and the microwave too—can make low-fire glazes chip or crack.

Low-fire glaze can only be applied to a project that has already been bisque-fired. Never put low-fire glazes on unfired pots, or greenware (wet, leather-hard, or bone-dry projects). If greenware is glaze-fired, it will blow up in the kiln and will likely damage someone else's project too.

Glazing Tip for Helpers

Be sure children wipe all glaze off the bottom of their projects with a damp sponge. When the project is fired, the glaze will melt. If there is glaze on the bottom of a project, the project will permanently stick to the kiln.

You Will Need:

- newspaper
- a completed project that has been bisque-fired
- nontoxic low-fire glazes
- a bucket for dipping glaze (optional)
- dipping tongs (optional)
- small sponge for wiping glaze from bottom of project
- paintbrushes and a toothbrush for applying glaze
- bowl of water to rinse your brushes
- a place to glaze-fire your work

GLAZING OVER UNDERGLAZE

If your project is underglazed and has been bisque-fired, you should apply clear low-fire glaze so your original underglaze design will show through. You can paint on 2 or 3 coats or dip-glaze your project as described on page 109. The result is a waterproof finish that can hold liquids after the project has been fired in the kiln.

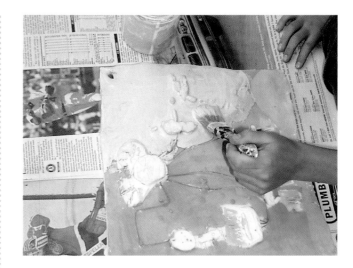

Austin paints on a clear glaze.

PAINTING WITH LOW-FIRE GLAZES

There are several ways to paint designs with low-fire glazes:

★ You can paint low-fire glaze with a brush onto bisque-fired projects, but the designs may not be as detailed as designs painted with underglaze.

★ You can add sponge designs by dipping a small sponge into glaze and pressing it against your bisque-fired project.

★ You can use a toothbrush to splatter glaze onto your bisque-fired project.

Mia demonstrates painting with low-fire glazes.

Dip-glazing is a quick way to evenly apply low-fire glaze to smaller projects that fit easily into a bucket. If you did not use underglazes on your bisque-fired project, you can use a color glaze. You can try one solid color, or dip different parts of your project into different colors. You will get interesting effects when the colors overlap. If you did use underglaze, use clear glaze so you'll be able to see your underglaze designs.

Lucy demonstrates dip-glazing.

1 Pour liquid glaze into a small bucket.

2 Lift your project over the bucket using the dipping tongs.

3 Quickly dip your project into the glaze then lift it out. If your project is a pot, remember to turn it upside down as you lift it so that glaze can run out of the pot and into the bucket.

4 Set your project on your work space right side up. It will be nearly dry.

5 When the glaze is completely dry, turn your project upside down.

6 Using a small damp sponge, wipe the glaze off the bottom of your project. This will keep your project from getting stuck to the bottom of the kiln when the glaze melts.

Burnishing

. . . .

Burnishing is an ancient technique for polishing clay by using a polished stone or a spoon and some oil. It gives the surface of your pot a high-gloss finish without using low-fire glazes.

Burnished and smoke-fired pot by Tess

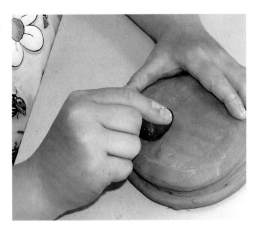

Erin uses a stone to burnish the bottom of her pot.

You Will Need:

- a leather-hard project
- a spoon or a polished stone to rub on the clay
- cooking oil to rub on the clay

BURNISHING

1 Take a polished stone or the back of a spoon and rub your pot when it's leather-hard. This closes the pores of the clay and leaves a shine on the surface.

2 When it's bone-dry, put a thin layer of vegetable oil on your pot and rub it with the stone or spoon again.

3 To keep its shine, the pot must be fired at a lower temperature. (Tell the lab technician that it should be fired between cone 018 and cone 012.)

Smoke Firing

Once your pot is bisque-fired, instead of low-fire glazing it you can smoke fire it for an ancient look. (This is sometimes called "pit firing.") Smoke firing is exciting, but should only be tried with adult help.

Smoke-fired pot by Abby

Smoke-Firing Tip for Helpers

Smoke-fired pots are for decorative use only and should not be used for food or for holding water. Different burnable materials will react slightly differently so smoke-firing requires some experimentation. For instance, colored newspaper will add color to projects. Straw or dry pine needles will make the project look textured. Projects will darken with repeated smoke-firings. Of course, this should only be done outdoors with adult supervision!

You Will Need:

- a bisque-fired project
- metal garbage can to burn newspaper, straw, or pine needles
- newspaper, straw, or dried pine needles to burn in the garbage can
- mesh screen with $1/4$-inch to $1/2$-inch grid to cover garbage can
- adult with matches

SMOKE FIRING

1 Find a safe, open area to put the metal garbage can.

2 Place 3 or 4 inches of newspaper strips, straw, or pine needles in the bottom of the garbage can. (Experiment with mixing these materials.)

TURN THE PAGE →

3 Place your bisque-fired project into the garbage can.

4 Cover your project with another 3-inch layer of torn newspaper strips and burnable materials.

5 Next, ask an adult to light the material on fire and cover the garbage can with the mesh screen. The carbon from the smoke will darken the surface of the pot.

6 Leave your pot in the garbage can for a couple of hours until it is cool to the touch.

CRACKED & BROKEN PIECES

There is no such thing as a mistake when you work with clay. —Danny

At some point, every ceramic artist has to face the difficult task of dealing with a cracked or a broken project. Maybe your project got dropped, bumped, or cracked in the kiln. When you work so hard on a project, it can be very upsetting when something appears to go wrong. Sadness, anger, and loss are all healthy feelings that may need to be expressed. But once the anger and the sadness are gone, you need to look at your project and explore your options. What would you like do with your cracked or broken project? Do you want to fix it, transform it into an abstract sculpture or a *mosaic*, or have you learned something that you'd like to try again? Whatever you decide to do, the next step is up to you.

Cracked pots are something that Kevin Nierman, founder of Kids 'N' Clay Pottery Studio, learned to deal with in his work as an artist. Today, he breaks his work on purpose and puts it back together to form interesting pots and sculptures. Kevin says:

"My first experience with clay was 25 years ago at a local private pottery studio. Breaking, cracking, or exploding projects in the kiln was common in my early years. My work never seemed to turn out the way I imagined. I remember how frustrated I used to get. But then I learned to accept my broken pots and realized that there was great beauty and character in what was happening. I would break my bisque-fired pots, glaze and fire the pieces separately, and then glue them back together. Once I started making my cracked pots, all my stiffness went away. The new forms seemed to express a deeper part of myself. Today, my cracked pots are shown in galleries across the country, and I've begun making a new series of wall sculptures.

Many of you may go through a similar discovery process when you first start working with clay. I know how challenging and disappointing it can be when a project breaks. But at the same time, it's also important to learn how to deal with loss and change, and how to adapt. Your feelings are important, but you must also pick up the pieces and go on. That might mean gluing the pieces, starting over, or just experiencing the process and letting the project go. The end result doesn't have to be a finished project. Working with clay is a lot like life. What you learn when you are making your project is the most valuable lesson, and discovering all the things you can do is what makes it fun."

Ceramic artist Kevin Nierman in front of one of his dramatic broken-pot wall sculptures

GLOSSARY OF CERAMIC TERMS

ASTM (American Society for Testing and Materials): This organization sets standards for hazardous labeling in art materials that are revised automatically every five years and more often if needed. Write them if you want a copy of the standards: ASTM, 1916 Race Street, Philadelphia, PA 19103.

Ashes: The grayish powder and unburned bits that are sometimes left inside hollow projects that were made with newspaper for support.

Bat: A $1/4$ inch to $3/4$ inch thick flat, wooden, or plastic disc that fits over the wheel-head of a potter's wheel. It's used to throw a pot on the wheel or to dry a pot when the bat is removed from the wheel. Sometimes it's square.

Bat pegs: The pegs on the wheel-head of a potter's wheel that hold the bat in place.

Bisque or bisqueware: Any unglazed or underglazed ceramic piece that has been fired at a low temperature before glazing. Bisqueware usually means something that has been bisque-fired in the kiln.

Bisque-firing: The first firing in the kiln at a low temperature (usually cone 010 to 04). This is how bisqueware is made.

Body (clay body): Any blend of clays and nonplastic ceramic materials that you can work with. Clay bodies are designed to become hard and ceramic at certain firing temperatures.

Bone-dry: A drying stage when your project is completely air dried and all the moisture is gone. Both white and red clay will become lighter and look "chalky."

Brushing: Applying slip or glaze using a paintbrush.

Burnishing: The process of polishing clay with a polished stone or spoon and some vegetable oil to give the surface of a pot a high-gloss finish without using glazes.

Canvas-covered board: A nonstick work surface made by covering a wooden board with canvas. Use tacks or staples from a staple gun to hold the canvas in place on the underside of the board.

Centering: A wheel-throwing skill that means shaping a ball of clay into an even form in the center of the spinning potter's wheel.

Centrifugal force: A force that tends to make spinning bodies (like clay walls) move away from the center.

Ceramics: Objects made from earthy materials that are transformed through a heat process. Also the process of making these objects.

Clay: A variety of earthy materials formed by the breakdown of granite rocks over millions of years. Can be combined with other materials to form different types of clay bodies.

Clay body: See Body.

Clear glaze: A clear coating that melts onto the clay surface with the use of heat. It will form a dull or glossy finish when fired to a certain temperature.

Coil: A long roll of clay that has been formed by hand. It should look like a snake.

Coiling: A handbuilding method that uses many coils to build walls, handles, etc. The coils are smoothed together to form a sturdy structure.

Collaring: A wheel-throwing method that prevents clay walls from expanding out (caused by centrifugal force). It is the act of pushing your cylinder walls gently toward the center.

Color glaze: A color coating that melts onto the clay surface with the use of heat. It will form a dull or glossy finish when fired to a certain temperature.

Cone: A small cone-shaped material that is sensitive to heat. It is placed inside the kiln so that lab workers will know exactly what the temperature levels are by watching when the cones melt.

Cracked pots: A term used to describe pots and projects that have been broken and put back together to form interesting designs and sculptures.

Cut-off tool: A tool used to cut off chunks of clay. It's a long piece of string attached to wooden handles on both ends.

Cylinder: A cylinder is a tube shape that is first formed on the potter's wheel after centering.

Decorative use only: A warning that a project should not be used for food or for holding liquid. It's only for looking at. These projects do not have a protective coating, so ceramic dust may get on food, and water will likely leak.

Dipping: A method of applying glaze to a project by dunking it in a bucket of glaze.

Drying: The natural removal of moisture from a project by the air. If you don't dry your project long enough before firing, it may crack or explode in the kiln.

Firing: The process of heating pottery and sculptures in a kiln or open fire.

Fettling knife: A carving knife with a narrow, round tip. It's used for cutting into leather-hard clay.

Foot: The base of a pot. The part that it stands on.

Foot pedal: The pedal on an electric potter's wheel that controls the speed of the spinning wheel.

Foundation: The bottom outside edge of a pot. Sometimes called the base.

Glaze: Any glass-like coating that melts onto the clay surface with the use of heat. It will form a dull or glossy finish when fired to a certain heat level.

Glaze firing: The second firing that heats and melts the glaze to form a glassy coating on the surface.

Greenware: Any unfired project that is leather-hard or bone-dry.

Handbuilding: A general term that means the process of making pottery and ceramic sculptures by hand, rather than on a potter's wheel. Usually refers to pinch, coil, and slab building methods.

Kick-wheel: A potter's wheel that is powered by kicking a rotating wheel with your foot.

Kiln: A special furnace or clay oven designed to safely increase heat from 0°F to 1944° F, or cone 04 (and more for high firings).

Leather-hard: A drying stage that occurs after your project has been air-dried about one day indoors, or as fast as 20 minutes in direct sunlight. The clay stiffens and holds its shape, but can still be easily carved.

Low-fire: Firing that does not exceed 1944° F, or cone 04.

Low-fire clay: Clay that is designed to become hard and ceramic at low-fire temperatures in the kiln.

Mold: Any hard form that can be used to shape a ceramic project.

Mosaic: Pictures or designs made from small bits of ceramics or small stones.

Neck: The narrow area of a pot below a flared opening.

Nichrome wire: A heat-resistant wire that will not melt in the kiln during firing.

Pinch or pinching: The handbuilding method of squeezing clay between your thumb and fingers to form a pot or sculpture.

Porcelain: A fine white translucent clay body that is more difficult to work with than low-fire clays.

Pot: In ceramics, any vessel or object made of clay.

Potter's wheel: A revolving wheel that is used to create pottery. It can be powered by foot or by electricity.

Pottery: Any ceramic object as well as the workshop where it is made.

Scoring: A method for attaching two pieces of clay by scratching the areas where they attach, applying slip, then smoothing and sealing the edges.

Sgraffito: An underglazing decorating method of scraping away a design into the underglaze on a project. This allows the clay body to show through. Ideal for use on leather-hard projects.

Shrinkage: As projects dry, the process of getting slightly smaller as the moisture leaves.

Slab: A handbuilding method that uses flat, even pieces of clay about 1/2 inch thick that are formed with a rolling pin.

Slip: A mixture of clay and water. It is used like glue as part of the scoring process. Can also be used for decorating.

Smoke firing: A decorative firing method that is used on bisque-fired projects. Flammable materials like newpaper, straw, or pine needles are put in a metal garbage can with the project, then lit on fire so the smoke can darken the surface of the pot.

Splash pan: The part of the potter's wheel where extra water and slushy clay is captured.

Trimming: The removal of extra clay off the foot or the body of wheel-thrown projects to refine the shape. This is done on the potter's wheel with a trimming tool.

Underglaze: Any coloring material used under a glaze. This is applied to greenware and then bisque-fired.

Underglaze pencils: Underglazes available in pencils, so detailed designs can be drawn directly on the project.

Wedging: The process of removing trapped air inside the clay by throwing a ball of clay on the canvas-covered board about 20 times. This is especially important when combining pieces of clay, recycling clay, or preparing clay for use on the potter's wheel.

Wheel-head: The part of the potter's wheel that rotates and spins.

BIBLIOGRAPHY

Bender, Sue. *Everyday Sacred: A Woman's Journey Home.* New York: Harper Collins, 1996.

Coakes, Michelle. *Creative Pottery: A Step-by-Step Guide and Showcase.* Gloucester, MA: Rockport Publishers, Inc., 1998.

Peterson, Susan. *The Craft and Art of Clay*, 2nd Ed. Englewood Cliffs, NJ: Prentice Hall, 1996.

Speight, Charlotte F. and John Toki. *Hands in Clay,* 4th Ed. Mountain View, CA: Mayfield Publishing Company, 1999.

Speight, Charlotte F. and John Toki. *Make It in Clay: A Beginner's Guide to Ceramics.* Mountain View, CA: Mayfield Publishing Company, 1997.